AF685930

INCORPORATION AND BUSINESS GUIDE FOR OREGON

INCORPORATION AND BUSINESS GUIDE FOR OREGON

How to form your own corporation

C. Thomas Davis, Attorney

Self-Counsel Press Inc.
a subsidiary of
International Self-Counsel Press Ltd.

Copyright © 1984, 1992 by Self-Counsel Press Inc.
All rights reserved.
No part of this book may be reproduced or transmitted in any form by any means — graphic, electronic, or mechanical — without permission in writing from the publisher, except by a reviewer who may quote brief passages in a review.

Printed in Canada

First edition: November, 1978;
Second edition: July, 1984
Third edition: April, 1988;
Fourth edition: December, 1992

Cataloging in Publication Data

Davis, C. Thomas, 1951-
Incorporation & business guide for Oregon

(Self-counsel legal series)
ISBN 0-88908-834-9

1. Incorporation — Oregon — Popular works. 2. Private companies — Oregon — Popular works. I. Title. II. Series.
KFO2613.5.Z9M34 1992 346.795'06622 C92-091721-6

Self-Counsel Press Inc.
a subsidiary of
International Self-Counsel Press Ltd.

1704 N. State Street
Bellingham, Washington
98225

1481 Charlotte Road
North Vancouver, British Columbia
Canada V7J 1H1

AVAILABLE FROM THE PUBLISHER

In order to incorporate you will need to file certain forms. You may type these yourself, but it is easier and quicker to use pre-printed forms. The pre-packaged forms are available where you bought this book or you may use the order form on page vi. The cost of the package is $12.95 plus tax and handling. The package includes:

3 sets Articles of Incorporation (1 working copy; 2 for filing)
2 Consents to Action of Board of Directors
2 Sets Bylaws
5 Share Certificates

ADDITIONAL ITEMS AVAILABLE FROM THE PUBLISHER

Company seal — the seal should not be ordered until you have received your Certificate of Incorporation, unless you are ordering the seal without the corporation name.
Seal with corporate name — **$31.50**

Minute book — $18.00 (A minute book is a loose-leaf binder designed to contain all your important corporate records, tabbed and indexed for easy use.)

Deposit stamp — "For Deposit Only to the Credit of ______ *(corporation name)* ______" — **$9.25**

Endorsement stamp — "Corporation Name" — $4.95

Corporation name and address stamp — 3 lines — **$8.95**
— 4 lines — **$10.95**

Extra share certificates — 30¢ each

Send to:
Self-Counsel Press Inc.
1704 N. State Street
Bellingham, WA 98225

(Clip and mail)

ORDER FORM

Please send the following items prepaid:

________	Package form kit	$12.95
________	Seal	31.50
________	Minute book	18.00
________	Deposit stamp	6.95
________	Endorsement stamp	4.95
________	Corporation name and address stamp — (3 lines)	8.95
	— (4 lines)	10.95
________	Extra share certificates — 30¢ each	________
	TOTAL	$ ________
	Add $2.00 for postage and handling	2.00
	Washington residents add 8.1% to total above for sales tax	________

TOTAL to be forwarded by money order, or billed to ❑ MasterCard ❑ Visa $ ________

MasterCard/Visa Number:________________ Expiry date:________

Signature:________________________________

Please send the items checked above to:

Mr./Ms. ________________________________

Address: ________________ City: ________________

State: ________________ Zip Code: ________________

Telephone: ________________________________

Name of corporation: ________________________________

Corporation address (for stamp) if not same as above): (Please Print) ________________

____

Prices subject to change without notice.

Please check your seals and stamps upon receipt.
We will not be responsible for errors reported more than 30 days after mailing.

CONTENTS

TABLES

SAMPLES

ACKNOWLEDGMENTS

The author wishes to acknowledge the assistance of Jerry Young, CPA, of Beaverton, Oregon, and Letty Owings, of Lake Oswego, Oregon.

NOTICE TO READERS

Laws are constantly changing. Every effort is made to keep this publication as current as possible. However, neither the author nor the publisher can accept any responsibility for changes to the law or practice that occur after the printing of this publication. Please be sure that you have the most recent edition.

Fee schedule citations are subject to change by the Oregon Legislature and the Corporation Division. You may obtain the most recent fee schedule by contacting the Corporation Division at (503) 378-4166.

Tax rates are also subject to constant change by the Congress and the Oregon Legislature. Please check with the Internal Revenue Service at (503) 221-3960, the Oregon Department of Revenue at (503) 371-2244, or a Certified Public Accountant (CPA).

1

WHY FORM A CORPORATION?

There are many good reasons for incorporating, but the purpose of this book is not to advise or encourage you to incorporate. Once you have made the decision to form a corporation, this book should help you meet the simple but exact requirements. The legislature of the state of Oregon has passed laws allowing you to form a legal business entity called a corporation. There are two types of corporations in Oregon:

(a) A stock corporation which —
   - (i) carries on business for profit,
   - (ii) distributes profits to shareholders, and
   - (iii) distributes its assets when dissolved.

(b) A non-stock, non-profit corporation which —
   - (i) is created for charitable, social, educational, religious, or cemetery purposes and
   - (ii) does not distribute profits to members or investors.

Most Oregon corporations are stock corporations with only a few shareholders. These small corporations are called "close corporations." This book is designed mainly to aid persons who are forming close corporations.

The basic procedure is simple. Where complex legal or accounting problems arise, it is a good idea to consult an attorney or accountant. This book will give you sufficient information about the law and about practical problems you will deal with. Where possible, forms which you need to fill out in the incorporation process are reproduced here.

Remember that you are not completely finished once you have created a corporation. You will still have to report to the state and file fees periodically during the existence of the corporation.

This book is not meant to replace the help of legal counsel. Although you can do the simpler steps yourself, you should be aware of areas in which you need legal counsel.

Before starting and investing in a business about which you know very little, it is imperative that you learn as much as you can about the business beforehand. Otherwise, it can prove to be an expensive and disturbing undertaking. If you are planning to go into a new business, my personal recommendation is that you first gain experience. Careful planning in advance of entering any business is most essential. Gain as much knowledge as you can because surprises can hurt. You might want to refer to *Starting a Successful Business on the West Coast,* another title in the Self-Counsel series. It is available from your local bookstores and explains all you need to know about state and federal licensing regulations and about financing and location.

As a starting point in planning your business you should answer the following questions:

(a) What kind of business are you thinking of?

(b) Who will manage it?

(c) Do you have a control and power structure in mind?

(d) Where will the business be located?

(e) How will you finance it?

(f) Is building, remodeling, or leasing required?

(g) What would be a good name?

(h) Who will be your competitors? What are their operations like? How do their businesses operate?

(i) What is your plan of operation? Are you modeling on others in your field or improving on their operation?

(j) Do you have a detailed budget planned and know what your cash flow will be?

Having the answers to these questions will be helpful in involving others in your business and in obtaining financing.

If you need business counseling, you may contact the

Small Business Advocate
Oregon Economic Development Dept.
595 Cottage Street, NE
Salem, OR 97310
(503) 373-1225

The Service Corps of Retired Executives (SCORE) is a counseling service for businesses. The Active Corps of Executives (ACE) is another organization designed to help small businesses. Members giving help are persons currently involved with a business. Both organizations may be contacted through the Small Business Administration.

2

METHODS OF CARRYING ON BUSINESS

You may be already engaged in a small business or be thinking about starting one, either by yourself or with someone else. One of the first decisions to be made is what your business form should be.

There are only three ways to carry on any business; these encompass every type of business, from the smallest corner grocery store to General Motors. If you are already carrying on business and are not incorporated, you must be operating either as a sole proprietorship or as a partner in a business. Another option is the corporation.

Special entities such as charities, limited partnerships and Massachusetts trusts will not be discussed in detail since they do not concern the typical small business.

a. THE SOLE PROPRIETORSHIP

The sole proprietorship form of business is the oldest, simplest, and least complicated type of business structure. It is simply an individual who engages in business for himself or herself.

The sole owner has absolute power to make decisions, delegate authority, and hire and fire employees.

The sole proprietor may sell or dispose of the business in any way he or she sees fit, at any time, without obtaining the agreement of another person. Or the proprietor may simply close the doors, liquidate the business assets and stop doing business. However, a sole proprietor is always personally responsible for paying debts and taxes and fulfilling all business obligations.

1. Advantages

The principal characteristic and advantage of the sole proprietorship is the absence of a formal business organization. There is no need to file formal papers of organization or enter into formal agreements with other parties. This enables a sole proprietor to avoid some of the regulations and costs imposed on corporations.

Another advantage of a sole proprietorship is the ability of the owner to make management decisions without interference from other parties. Also, the sole owner does not risk liabilities for debts created by others.

The sole proprietor will also avoid the double tax on earnings distributed to owner-shareholders of corporations. This situation arises when a corporation must first pay tax on its net earnings and then the shareholders must pay tax on dividends they receive. Working partners who earn salaries must pay tax on that money as well.

2. Disadvantages

The major disadvantage to the sole proprietorship is that the sole proprietor is personally responsible for the performance of all contracts, the fulfillment of all business obligations, and the payment of all debts and taxes incurred in the operation of the business. All of the sole owner's personal assets may be seized for the payment of business obligations and taxes; however, all profits belong to him or her.

Unless the sole owner has insurance that legally limits liability for fire, theft, product liability, and personal injury claims, he or she will be personally liable for the full amount in case of a loss.

Also, the sole proprietor is personally responsible and liable for all of the acts of his or her employees in the performance of their work. The employer-employee relationship is called a "principal and agent" relationship. The sole owner is the principal; the employees are agents.

An example of this is where an employee operates an automobile, owned either by the employer or by the employee, and in the course of the employer's business he or she causes an accident through negligent driving. The employer as well as the employee is liable for damages. For protection, the sole owner should carry adequate public liability insurance including nonowned automobile insurance. Workers' Compensation insurance must also be carried.

Employees acting within the scope of their authorized duties can make their employer responsible for carrying out the terms of an oral or written contract whether or not their employer consents or approves of the terms.

In addition, the sole owner is also personally responsible for the payment of all social security taxes, withholding taxes, federal and state unemployment insurance, industrial insurance premiums, and medical and pension plan premiums that are deducted from employees' wages, as well as for making his or her own contribution to these various plans.

A further disadvantage of the sole proprietorship is that the owner has only personal resources to invest in or to expand the business.

Any profits of the business are taxed as an ordinary income to the owner and he or she is not entitled to the fringe benefits afforded corporate employees under our tax laws.

Finally, since the business is subject to disintegration upon the death or incapacity of the owner, estate planning can become complex.

3. Doing business under a name other than your own

As sole proprietor, you are not required to conduct business under your own name. An assumed or trade business name may be used as long as it is not in conflict with any existing trade business name. You may wish to use a name descriptive of your business or locale, or you may simply want to avoid the use of your own name. To use an assumed name, you must register it with the state Corporation Commissioner. The application fee is $10.00 plus an additional $1.50 for each county in which you wish to use the name. Send the fee, with the registration form (see Sample #1), to —

Corporation Commissioner
Commerce Building
158 12th Street, N.E.
Salem, Oregon 97310-0210

Remember to enter the Standard Industrial Classification (SIC) code from the back of the application that most closely describes the nature of your business.

If you are not going to use an assumed name, you do not need to register.

b. GENERAL PARTNERSHIPS

1. What is a partnership?

This section will explain the formation, nature, characteristics, rights, obligations and dissolution of general partnerships. Limited partnerships and joint ventures will be discussed in the next section.

A partnership is defined as an association of two or more persons who operate a business for profit. Like a proprietorship, a partnership is not a separate legal entity apart from its partners or members. It is an association of two or more persons who have agreed to engage in a business venture.

A general partnership is created by an agreement that can be oral, written, or implied.

A general partnership agreement is not required by law to be in writing, and it

SAMPLE #1
ASSUMED BUSINESS NAME REGISTRATION

Fee: $10.00
+ 2.00 per county
TOTAL: ____________

STATE OF OREGON
CORPORATION DIVISION
158 12th Street NE
Salem, OR 97310

Registry Number:

ASSUMED BUSINESS NAME REGISTRATION

____
(Office Use Only)

PLEASE COMPLETE ALL SECTIONS LEGIBLY IN BLACK INK

1. **ASSUMED BUSINESS NAME:** Suds Shop

2. Principal Place of Business: 30 Clean Street Anytown, Oregon 00000
Street and Number City State Zip Code

3. Authorized Representative (**ONE NAME ONLY**): John Doe
30 Clean Street Anytown Oregon 00000
Street and Number or PO Box City State Zip Code

4. SIC Code: ____________

5. Registrants (attach a separate sheet if necessary):

Name: ____________ Name: ____________
Street Address: ____________ Street Address: ____________
____________ ____________

Name: ____________ Name: ____________
Street Address: ____________ Street Address: ____________
____________ ____________

6. Counties: ____ All Counties (statewide registration)

____ Baker	____ Douglas	____ Lake	____ Sherman
____ Benton	____ Gilliam	____ Lane	____ Tillamook
____ Clackamas	____ Grant	____ Lincoln	____ Umatilla
____ Clatsop	____ Harney	____ Linn	____ Union
____ Columbia	____ Hood River	____ Malheur	____ Wallowa
____ Coos	X Jackson	____ Marion	____ Wasco
____ Crook	____ Jefferson	____ Morrow	____ Washington
____ Curry	____ Josephine	____ Multnomah	____ Wheeler
____ Deschutes	____ Klamath	____ Polk	____ Yamhill

7. Signature of all registrants (attach a separate sheet if necessary):

____________ ____________
____________ ____________

. Person to contact about this registration: John Doe

Daytime telephone number: 000-0000

ABN NEW (6/87) 831.115 ($ ________)

Note: You are the authorized representative.

SAMPLE #1
(Back)

Standard Industrial Classification (S.I.C.) Code List

After reading through the following list, select the four-digit number that most closely identifies your type of business. Write that four-digit number in the space provided on your form.

DIVISION A. AGRICULTURE, FORESTRY, & FISHING

0100 Agricultural Production-Crops
0200 Agricultural Production-Livestock
0700 Agricultural Services
0800 Forestry
0910 Commercial Fishing
0920 Fish Hatcheries & Preserves
0970 Hunting, Trapping & Game Propagation

DIVISION B. MINING

1000 Metal Mining
1100 Anthracite Mining
1200 Bituminous Coal & Lignite Mining
1300 Oil & Gas Extraction
1400 Nonmetallic Minerals Including Stone, Sand & Gravel

DIVISION C. CONSTRUCTION

1520 General Building Contractors — Residential Buildings
1530 Operative Builders Who Construct & Sell Buildings On Their Own Account Rather Than As Contractors
1540 General Building Contractors — Nonresidential Buildings
1610 Highway & Street Construction
1620 Heavy Construction
1710 Plumbing, Heating (except Electric) & Air Conditioning
1720 Painting, Paper Hanging & Decorating
1730 Electrical Work
1740 Masonry, Stonework, Tile Setting & Plastering
1750 Carpentering & Flooring
1760 Roofing & Sheet Metal Work
1770 Concrete Work
1780 Water Well Drilling
1790 Special Trade Contractors Not Otherwise Listed Above

DIVISION D. MANUFACTURING

2010 Meat Products
2020 Dairy Products
2030 Canned & Preserved Fruits & Vegetables
2040 Grain Mill Products
2050 Bakery Products
2060 Sugar & Confectionery Products
2070 Fats & Oils
2080 Beverages
2090 Food Preparations & Products
2100 Tobacco Manufacturers
2200 Textile Mill Products
2300 Apparel & Other Finished Products
2400 Lumber & Wood Products
2500 Furniture & Fixtures
2600 Paper & Allied Products
2700 Printing & Publishing
2810 Industrial Inorganic Chemicals
2820 Plastics Materials & Synthetics
2830 Drugs
2840 Soap, Detergents & Cleaning Preparations
2850 Paints, Varnishes & Allied Products
2860 Industrial Organic Chemicals
2870 Agricultural Chemicals
2890 Chemical Products Not Otherwise Listed Above
2910 Petroleum Refining
2950 Paving & Roofing Materials
2990 Products of Petroleum & Coal
3000 Rubber & Misc. Plastics Products
3100 Leather Tanning & Finishing & Leather Products
3200 Stone, Clay, Glass & Concrete Products
3300 Primary Metal Industries
3400 Fabricated Metal Products
3500 Machinery, Except Electrical
3600 Electrical & Electronic Machinery, Equipment & Supplies
3710 Motor Vehicles & Motor Vehicle Equipment
3720 Aircraft & Parts
3730 Ship & Boat Building & Repairing
3740 Railroad Equipment
3750 Motorcycles, Bicycles & Parts
3760 Guided Missiles, Space Vehicles & Parts
3790 Transportation Equipment Not Otherwise Listed Above
3800 Measuring, Analyzing & Controlling Instruments; Photographic, Medical & Optical Goods; Watches & Clocks
3910 Jewelry, Silverware & Plated Ware
3930 Musical Instruments
3940 Toys & Amusement, Sporting & Athletic Goods
3950 Pens, Pencils & Other Office & Artists' Materials
3960 Costume Jewelry, Novelties, Buttons & Notions
3990 Manufacturing Industries Not Otherwise Listed Above

DIVISION E. TRANSPORTATION, COMMUNICATIONS, ELECTRIC, GAS & SANITARY SERVICES

4000 Railroad Transportation
4110 Local & Suburban Passenger Transportation
4120 Taxicabs
4130 Intercity & Rural Highway Passenger Transportation
4140 Passenger Transportation Charter Service
4170 Terminal & Service Facilities for Motor Vehicle Passenger Transportation
4210 Trucking, Local & Long Distance
4220 Public Warehousing
4230 Terminal & Joint Terminal Maintenance Facilities for Motor Freight Transportation
4400 Water Transportation
4500 Transportation by Air
4600 Pipelines, Except Natural Gas
4700 Transportation Services Not Otherwise Listed Above
4810 Telephone Communication (Wire or Radio)
4820 Telegraph Communication (Wire or Radio)
4830 Radio & Television Broadcasting
4890 Communication Services Not Otherwise Listed Above
4910 Electric Services
4920 Gas Production & Distribution
4930 Combination Electric & Gas & Other Utility Services
4940 Water Supply
4950 Sanitary Services
4960 Steam Supply
4970 Irrigation Systems

DIVISION F. WHOLESALE TRADE

5010 Motor Vehicles, Automotive Parts & Supplies
5020 Furniture & Home Furnishings
5030 Lumber & Other Construction Materials
5040 Sporting, Recreational, Photographic & Hobby Goods & Toys & Supplies
5050 Metals & Minerals, Except Petroleum
5060 Electrical Goods
5070 Hardware, Plumbing & Heating Equipment & Supplies
5080 Machinery, Equipment & Supplies
5090 Durable Goods Not Otherwise Listed Above
5110 Paper & Paper Products
5120 Drugs, Proprietaries & Sundries
5130 Apparel, Piece Goods & Notions
5140 Groceries & Related Products
5150 Farm-Product Raw Materials
5160 Chemicals & Allied Products
5170 Petroleum & Petroleum Products
5180 Beer, Wine & Distilled Alcoholic Beverages
5190 Nondurable Goods Not Otherwise Listed Above

DIVISION G. RETAIL TRADE

5200 Building Materials Dealers (Including Lumber, Hardware & Mobile Home Dealers)
5300 General Merchandise Stores
5400 Food Stores Including Candy Stores
5510 Motor Vehicle Dealers (New & Used)
5520 Motor Vehicle Dealers (Used Only)
5530 Auto & Home Supply Stores
5540 Gasoline Service Stations
5550 Boat Dealers
5560 Recreation & Utility Trailer Dealers
5570 Motorcycle Dealers
5590 Automotive Dealers Not Otherwise Listed Above
5600 Apparel & Accessory Stores
5700 Furniture, Home Furnishings & Equipment Stores
5800 Eating & Drinking Places
5910 Drug Stores & Proprietary Stores
5920 Liquor Stores
5930 Used Merchandise Stores
5940 Retail Goods Stores Such As Sporting Goods, Bicycles, Books, Stationery, Jewelry & Hobby Stores
5960 Nonstore Retailers
5980 Fuel & Ice Dealers
5990 Retail Stores Not Otherwise Listed Above

DIVISION H. FINANCE, INSURANCE & REAL ESTATE

6000 Banking
6100 Credit Agencies Other Than Banks
6200 Security & Commodity Brokers, Dealers, Exchanges & Services
6300 Insurance Including Insurance Carriers Of All Types
6400 Insurance Agents, Brokers & Service
6500 Real Estate Including Cemeteries
6600 Any Combination of Real Estate, Insurance, Loans & Law Offices
6710 Holding Offices Which Hold Or Own Securities For The Purpose Of Exercising Some Degree Of Control Over Companies
6720 Investment Offices
6730 Trusts Consisting Of Establishments Primarily Engaged In The Management Of The Funds Of Individual Trusts & Foundations
6790 Investors Such As Oil Royalty Traders, Patent Owners & Investment Clubs

DIVISION I. SERVICES

7000 Hotels, Rooming Houses, Camps & Other Lodging Places
7210 Laundry, Cleaning & Garment Services
7220 Photographic Studios (Portrait)
7230 Beauty Shops & Barber Shops
7250 Shoe Repair, Shoe Shine & Hat Cleaning Shops
7260 Funeral Service & Crematories
7290 Personal Services
7310 Advertising
7320 Credit Reporting, Mercantile Reporting & Adjustment & Collection Agencies
7330 Mailing, Reproduction, Commercial Art & Photography & Stenographic Services
7340 Services to Dwellings & Other Buildings
7350 News Syndicates
7360 Personnel Supply Services
7370 Computer & Data Processing Services
7510 Automobile Rental & Leasing
7520 Automobile Parking
7530 Auto Repair Shops
7540 Automotive Services, except Repair
7620 Electrical Repair Shops
7630 Watch, Clock & Jewelry Repair
7640 Reupholstery & Furniture Repair
7690 Repair Shops Not Otherwise Listed Above
7810 Motion Picture Production & Distribution & Allied Services
7830 Motion Picture Theaters
7910 Dance Halls, Studios & Schools
7920 Theatrical Producers
7930 Bowling Alleys & Billiard & Pool Establishments
7940 Commercial Sports
7990 Amusement & Recreation Services Not Otherwise Listed Above
8010 Offices Of Licensed Physicians
8020 Offices of Licensed Dentists
8030 Offices of Licensed Osteopathic Physicians
8040 Offices of Other Health Practitioners
8050 Nursing & Personal Care Facilities
8060 Hospitals
8070 Medical & Dental Laboratories
8080 Outpatient Care Facilities
8090 Health & Allied Services Not Otherwise Listed Above
8100 Legal Services
8200 Educational Services Such As Libraries, Schools, Including Nondegree Granting Schools, Except Dancing Schools
8320 Individual & Family Social Services
8330 Job Training & Related Social Services
8350 Child Day Care Services
8360 Residential Care
8380 Senior Citizens Associations
8390 Social Services Not Otherwise Listed Above
8400 Museums, Botanical & Zoological Gardens
8610 Business Associations
8620 Professional Associations
8630 Labor Organizations
8640 Civic & Social Associations
8650 Political Organizations
8660 Religious Organizations
8680 Farm Granges
8910 Engineering & Architectural Services
8920 Noncommercial Research Organizations
8930 Accounting, Auditing & Bookkeeping
8990 Services Not Otherwise Listed Such As Lecturers, Authors, & Artists
0000 Not Yet Organized Or Inactive

may simply be an oral understanding (that is sometimes evidenced by a handshake) followed by performance of the terms of the understanding. However, it is *strongly recommended* that the agreement of the partners be put in writing and signed by all partners. When a partnership agreement is in writing there is a better understanding of —

(a) the business purposes of the general partnership,
(b) the organization of the business,
(c) the duties and authority of each partner,
(d) the amount of capital each partner has invested in the business (this is called the participating percentage),
(e) the sharing of profits,
(f) the termination of the general partnership, and
(g) the transfer of interest from departing partners to remaining partners.

It is important to realize that you may be considered to be in partnership with someone even though you have made no formal declaration of such a partnership. A partnership can be created by the relationship of the parties, not just by formal agreement.

Unless a formal partnership document exists, there is no single established test as to what constitutes a partnership. The following factors are guidelines in determining whether or not it is a partnership:

(a) Is there a sharing of profits and losses?
(b) Do any of the parties act as agents for others?
(c) Is there any property held in joint tenancy?
(d) Is there any implication of partnership on your firm's letterhead or in its correspondence?
(e) Is the nature of the working relationship that of a partnership?
(f) Do the parties deal with the public or "hold themselves out" as partners?

2. Advantages

The most important advantage of a partnership is sharing knowledge, ability and experience. The partnership as a whole gains from drawing upon the strengths and financial resources of each partner.

3. Disadvantages

The chief danger of doing business as a general partnership is the risk of *unlimited partnership liability* that each individual partner assumes.

The property of the general partnership is available for the payment of all the debts and obligations incurred by the general partnership and all the taxes owed. If the general partnership property is insufficient to pay the debts, obligations, and taxes of the general partnership, then each of the partners becomes *personally* responsible for paying *all* the debts, obligations, and taxes.

This means that a partner, as an individual, becomes liable for the entire amount owed by the general partnership and not just a proportionate share of the debts, obligations, and taxes. However, it is only after the general partnership assets have been exhausted that the individual partners personally may be compelled to pay.

In such a case, each partner's personal assets become vulnerable to satisfy a judgment against the general partnership and the partners. In addition, each individual partner is personally responsible for the business actions of all partners acting on behalf of the general partnership.

4. Rights and obligations of partners

All the partners have equal rights in the management and conduct of the general partnership business, but the general partnership agreement should specify details about the authority and duties of each. Without a clear statement of the authority and duties assigned to each of the individual partners, misunderstanding and confusion can easily result.

No partner is entitled to receive a salary or wages for acting on behalf of the general partnership unless the general partnership agreement specifies such payments or the partner is engaged as an employee. Each partner has the right to inspect and examine the books of the general partnership at any reasonable time, regardless of personal authority or duties. Each partner is entitled to the repayment, at the time agreed upon, of loans made on behalf of the general partnership.

5. The partnership agreement

A general partnership agreement should state the following:

(a) The name of the general partnership
(b) The names and addresses of all partners
(c) The type of business planned
(d) The address of the business
(e) The date the partnership began
(f) The expected duration of the partnership
(g) The cash and property each partner has invested in the partnership
(h) The amount each partner will pay if more capital is needed
(i) The duties and services of each partner
(j) The salary of each partner if there is a salary
(k) The fact that each partner's drawing account will be deducted from his or her share of the profits.
(l) The division of profits and losses

6. How is a partnership dissolved?

The law says that a partnership dissolves automatically on the death, retirement, or insanity of a partner, unless other provisions are made in the general partnership agreement.

The general partnership agreement may provide for continuance of the partnership regardless of any of the above causes of dissolution except bankruptcy or a court decree dissolving the partnership.

Upon the election of the partners to dissolve the general partnership, it will continue to exist after such action has been taken until all the affairs have been settled and the debts paid. The agreement or election to dissolve the partnership does not relieve the partners from the possibility of individual personal liability for the payment of the general partnership's debts and taxes.

Winding up the affairs of the general partnership means that its obligations must be settled, its debts and taxes paid, and its remaining assets distributed to the partners or personal representatives of a deceased partner.

All creditors of the general partnership should know of the dissolution. Send a letter to each creditor stating that it has been dissolved and that no person has authority to act or to incur obligations for the general partnership.

c. LIMITED PARTNERSHIPS

1. What are they?

A limited partnership is a partnership of one or more general partners and one or more limited partners. The purpose of a limited partnership is to allow persons to invest their money without being liable as general partners for all debts of the partnership. This gives a limited partner limited liability comparable to that of a corporate shareholder. In other words, the limited partner is not personally liable for the debts of the partnership.

Limited partners can lose only their investment in the business. A limited partner is not liable unless he or she takes part in the control of the business. In other words, a limited partner, at the risk of being held liable as a general partner, may not in any way participate in the management or control of the partnership business.

The Uniform Limited Partnership Act has specific regulations concerning the firm name. A limited partner's surname cannot be used as part of the business name. If it is, he or she will be liable as a general partner to creditors.

Generally, partners in a limited partnership share equally in profits and losses. However, a partner's share in the profits and losses and the partnership interests of the partners may be unequal. The limited partnership agreement should specify each partner's proportionate share of profits and losses.

The assets of the partnership belong to the limited partnership as a whole. During the life of the partnership, the individual partners do not, as such, have the right to ownership to specific assets of the partnership; each owns his or her proportionate interest in the property of the limited partnership.

When the partnership is dissolved, each partner is entitled to receive his or her share of the partnership property. If the partners cannot agree on how to divide the assets, the court can decide. This may be expensive, however.

Under the Uniform Limited Partnership Act, a corporation may act as a general partner. Because of the similarity to a limited partnership investment in corporate stock, there is always the danger that a limited partnership will be treated as an "association" that is taxable as a corporation. If you are contemplating a limited partnership arrangement with a corporate general partner, you should apply for an advance ruling from the IRS (Internal Revenue Service) on whether or not your limited partnership is a partnership for federal tax purposes.

2. How to form a limited partnership

Unlike a general partnership, which is not required by law to have an agreement in writing or to comply with any particular formalities, the limited partnership must comply strictly with the requirements of Oregon law stated in ORS 69.180. All general partners and limited partners must be designated as either general or limited partners. Each must sign and acknowledge the certificate of limited partnership. The certificate must state the following:

(a) The name of the partnership

(b) The character of the business

(c) The location of the principal place of business

(d) The address of the initial registered office and the name of the initial registered agent

(e) The term for which the partnership is to exist

(f) The amount of cash and the agreed value of other property contributed by each limited partner, together with a description of such property

(g) The additional contributions, if any, each limited partner agrees to make and the times at which they shall be made

(h) The time, if agreed upon, when the contribution of each limited partner is to be returned

(i) The share of the profits or other compensation by way of income which each limited partner shall receive by reason of his or her contribution

(j) The right, if given, of a limited partner to substitute an assignee as a contributor and the terms and conditions of the substitution

(k) The right, if given, of the limited partners to admit additional limited partners

(l) The right, if given, of one or more of the limited partners to priority over other limited partners, as to repayment of contributions or as to compensation by way of income and the nature of such priority

(m) The right, if given, of limited partners to demand and receive property other than cash in return for their contributions

(n) The right, if given, of the remaining general partner or general partners to continue the business on the death, retirement, incapacity, or insanity of a general partner

(o) The right, if given, of limited partners to demand and receive property other than cash in return for their contribution

(p) The right, if given, of a limited partner to vote on any of the matters described in ORS 69.280 and the vote required for election or removal of general partners

Because the formation, preparation, and conduct of a limited partnership is complicated and technical, it is recommended that an attorney be retained to prepare the certificate of limited partnership and to advise the general and limited partners of their rights, duties, obligations, and limitations.

Once the certificate is prepared, you must file a signed and verified copy at the office of the Corporate Commissioner. An example is shown in Sample #2. The filing fee, license, and surcharge fees total $40. Ask the Commissioner for a receipt, and keep it in your files to prove that you have filed the certificate. You should keep the second copy of the certificate in the partnership files.

3. How to dissolve a limited partnership

A limited partnership is like a general partnership in that the death, retirement or insanity of a general partner will automatically dissolve a limited partnership unless other provisions are made in the certificate. The certificate of limited partnership may also provide the time for which the limited partnership shall exist and the date when it will automatically dissolve. Whenever a limited partnership is dissolved, its affairs must be settled; its debts, obligations, and taxes paid; and the remaining cash and other assets distributed. Distribution is made first to limited partners in accordance with their proportionate shares; the balance of the cash and other assets is then distributed to the general partners. When a limited partnership dissolves, the certificate of limited partnership must be canceled. A letter of cancellation, signed by all the partners, and a filing fee of $20 must be filed in the office of the Corporation Commissioner.

An attorney should be retained to guide the limited partnership in the procedures necessary to terminate its existence.

d. JOINT VENTURE

A joint venture is an association of persons joined together to conduct a temporary business or single business transaction, or a series of separate single business transactions, with an agreement to share profits and losses. A joint venture differs from a general partnership in that the general partnership plans to engage in a continuing business. A joint venture is similar to a general partnership in that each of the joint venturers is subject to and equally responsible for all of the debts, obligations, and taxes of the joint venture.

e. ALL ABOUT CORPORATIONS

1. Introduction

A corporation is defined as "a legal entity, artificial or fictitious, existing only in contemplation of law." It is a separate entity apart from its incorporators, officers, directors, shareholders or employees. As a separate entity it has special powers defined by law. In Oregon, a corporation can do just about anything a natural person can do. A corporation comes into existence when its Articles of Incorporation have been accepted and filed in the office of the Corporation Commissioner.

A stock corporation is one organized to carry on a business for profit, to distribute profits as dividends to its shareholders, and to distribute its assets to shareholders when it is dissolved.

Another type of corporation commonly formed in Oregon is the nonstock or nonprofit corporation, which does not distribute its gains or profits to its members. It is a corporation in which individuals associate themselves together for religious, charitable, social, educational or cemetery purposes, or for rendering services subject to laws and regulations applicable to the particular class of nonprofit corporation or line of activity.

SAMPLE #2
CERTIFICATE OF LIMITED PARTNERSHIP

Submit the original
and one true copy
$40.00

Registry Number: ______________

SECRETARY OF STATE
Corporation Division
Business Registry
158 12th Street NE
Salem, OR 97310-0210
(503) 378-4166

THIS SPACE FOR OFFICE USE ONLY

CERTIFICATE OF LIMITED PARTNERSHIP

PLEASE TYPE OR PRINT LEGIBLY IN BLACK INK

1. Name of limited partnership: Cream Puff Bakers Limited Partnership

   NOTE: Must contain the words "limited partnership" without abbreviation.

2. Latest date upon which the partnership is to dissolve: Five days (or months, years)

3. Address of the office where records of the partnership will be kept:

   30 Sweet Street — Anytown — **Oregon** — 00000
   Must be an **Oregon street** address — City — Zip code

4. Name and street address of initial registered agent: Peter Fudge
   Name

   444 Nutty Boulevard — Anytown — **Oregon** — 00000
   Must be an **Oregon street** address — City — Zip code

5. Address where the Division may mail notices: (C/O:) (Attn:) John Cupcake

   222 Cherry Drive — Anytown — — 00000
   Street and number or PO box — City — State — Zip code

6. Name and business address of each general partner:

Linda Strawberry	John Cupcake
333 Donut Drive	222 Cherry Drive
City, Oregon 00000	Anytown, Oregon 00000

7. Optional provisions (attach a separate sheet if necessary):

8. Signature of each general partner:

   Linda Strawberry — John Cupcake

9. Person to contact about this filing: Peter Fudge — 000-0000
   Name — Daytime phone number

Make checks payable to the Corporation Division. Submit the completed form and fee to: Corporation Division, Business Registry, 158 12th Street NE, Salem, Oregon 97310-0210.

The majority of Oregon stock corporations are "close stock corporations" which means that the stock is owned by one person or a small number of people and these same people are also directors. This type of corporation is the principal subject of this book.

The major advantage of the corporate form is the limited liability of the shareholders for the debts of the business. Generally a shareholder's risk of loss is limited to the amount invested in the corporation, and the debts of the corporation cannot be satisfied by the personal assets of the shareholder. Ownership in a public corporation is freely transferable by the sale and transfer of stock certificates. Shares in a "close" corporation are also transferable but may have certain restrictions attached to their transfer. Unlike a sole proprietorship or a partnership, the existence of the corporation is perpetual and will not cease upon the death or incapacity of any shareholder.

Some of the disadvantages of a corporation relate to the ease of transfer of ownership. Because ownership can be transferred so easily, incompatible investors may become co-owners of the business. This is particularly true in a small, closely held corporation. But such a problem may be solved through the use of a buy-sell agreement (see chapter 7 for details). Since the corporation is a creature of law, it is subject to state regulatory and reporting requirements and tax laws. As such, it must qualify to do business in each foreign jurisdiction (i.e., state).

Corporations must pay extra organizational costs and fees required by law, payable to the Corporation Commissioner. Also, yearly fees have to be paid to keep the corporation in good standing. (See chapter 10 on Annual Reports for details.)

By following the recommendations and directions in this book and adapting its examples of forms and letters to your needs, you should be able to form your own close corporation with a minimum of expense and a minimum of legal assistance.

In each kind of business structure, except that of the limited partnership, the most important consideration to the investor is the risk of loss of the investment and his or her personal liability for payment of debts. In the general partnership and joint venture, each general partner or joint venturer becomes responsible for the payment of debts and taxes in proportion to the number of participants in the entity. Therefore, to avoid the risk of unlimited liability and to enjoy advantages not available to the other business structures, form your own corporation.

2. Where to incorporate

Since a corporation is an artificial person in the eyes of the law, it must be "born" or incorporated in the state where it starts into business. Following expansion it can be registered in other states to qualify to do business as a "foreign" corporation in those states. Once you expand outside your home state, you must follow the registration procedure for every state where you intend to do business.

Note: What constitutes "doing business" in a foreign state is often a complex issue. For example, setting up an office in Seattle would certainly mean your corporation would need to be registered in Washington. However, if you merely order goods from out of state on a regular basis, it probably would not constitute "doing business" in that particular state *unless* your corporation took delivery in that state or you had to sue the supplier in the courts of that state. Remember that in order to become legally recognized in any state other than the one in which you incorporated, you are required to register your corporation. Registration requirements are something to watch out for and to be aware of *at all times.*

3. Who may incorporate?

Any person or group of persons over the age of 18 may act as incorporators by completing and filing the required articles with the Corporation Commissioner's office and by paying the proper fees.

4. What can a corporation do?

Because a corporation is an artificial person and created from law, it has to be given the authority or power to do certain things. The Oregon Business Corporation Act gives every Oregon corporation the following powers.

57.030 General powers. Each corporation shall have power:

(1) To have perpetual succession by its corporate name unless a limited period of duration is stated in its articles of incorporation.

(2) To sue and be sued, complain and defend, in its corporate name.

(3) To have a corporate seal which may be altered at pleasure, and to use the same by causing it, or a facsimile thereof, to be impressed or affixed or in any other manner reproduced.

(4) To purchase, take, receive, lease, or otherwise acquire, own, hold, improve, use and otherwise deal in and with, real or personal property, or any interest therein, wherever situated.

(5) To sell, convey, mortgage, pledge, lease, exchange, transfer and otherwise dispose of all or any part of its property and assets.

(6) To lend money and use its credit to assist its employees and directors.

(7) To purchase, take, receive, subscribe for, or otherwise acquire, own, hold, vote, use, employ, sell, mortgage, lend, pledge, or otherwise dispose of, and otherwise use and deal in and with, shares or other interests in, or obligations of, other domestic or foreign corporations, associations, partnerships or individuals, or direct or indirect obligations of the United States or of any other government, state, territory, governmental district or municipality or of any instrumentality thereof.

(8) To make contracts and guarantees and incur liabilities, borrow money at such rates of interest as the corporation may determine, issue its notes, bonds and other obligations, and secure any of its obligations by mortgage or pledge of all or any of its property, franchises and income.

(9) To lend money for its corporate purposes, invest and reinvest its funds and take and hold real and personal property as security for the payment of funds so loaned or invested.

(10) To conduct its business, carry on its operations, and have offices and exercise the powers granted by this chapter within or without this state.

(11) To elect or appoint officers and agents of the corporation, and define their duties and fix their compensation.

(12) To make and alter bylaws, not inconsistent with its articles of incorporation or with the laws of this state, for the administration and regulation of the affairs of the corporation.

(13) To make donations for the public welfare or for charitable, scientific or educational purposes.

(14) To transact any lawful business which the board of directors shall find will be in the aid of governmental policy.

(15) To pay pensions and establish pension plans, pension trusts, profit-sharing plans, stock bonus plans and other incentive plans for any or all of its directors, officers or employees.

(16) To cease its corporate activities and surrender its corporate franchise.

(17) To be a promoter, partner, member, associate or manager of any partnership, joint venture, trust or other enterprise.

(18) To have and exercise all powers necessary or convenient to effect any of or all the purposes for which the corporation is organized.

5. How does a corporation work?

If you were to visualize the structure of a corporation, it would appear as follows:

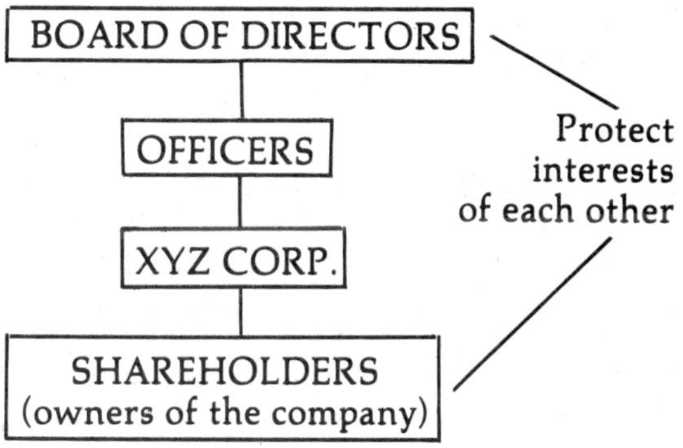

In theory, all corporations look like this diagram. In practice, there is a vast difference between public (reporting) corporations as opposed to incorporated partnerships or small family-owned (non-reporting) corporations.

Non-reporting companies can be more accurately described as "close corporations" rather than as corporations as we normally view them, because they usually consist of one, two, or three people who are close personal friends or business associates or family members.

Reporting companies differ in that the directors, officers, and shareholders are usually separate individuals. The directors on the board of a reporting company usually consist of a group of business people, respected in the community, who bring to the board a wide variety of business experience. Their function is to act as "watchdogs" over the officers and to protect the shareholders' interests.

Unfortunately, for a variety of reasons, this objective is not always attained. Most officers of large reporting companies are "hired professionals" and they are in charge of the day-to-day activities. In many instances they also wield great influence on the overall operations of the company. Usually the two or three top officers of the company are also members of the board of directors. The largest group in a reporting company consists of the shareholders, and this group is the theoretical "owner" of the company which, in turn, owns the assets. Shares represent "power" in relation to the company and its operations.

In theory, final authority and power for corporate actions is held by the shareholders, but this may be a myth for several reasons. The shareholders may be widely dispersed geographically with only a few of them able to attend the annual meeting. Also, most people do not buy shares on a stock exchange in the hope of participating in the internal workings of the company. They are after two things only — return (dividends) and appreciation in the value of their shares. If they become disillusioned, they do not seek to have management or directors replaced; they simply sell out. In addition, not too many people are knowledgeable enough to have a clear idea of how the day-to-day operations actually work. They are not, therefore, in a position to question the activities of management or the board of directors. A great deal of time, money, and effort is required for an individual, or group of individuals, to gain enough support to seriously challenge the members of the board of directors and management.

Be careful not to confuse the positions of shareholder, officer, and director even through the persons occupying them are the same. In a close corporation you are often wearing more than one hat at the same time.

To illustrate, in the day-to-day activities of your small business, you are an officer. If you decide, however, to branch out into a new area or to purchase or sell assets, you will be a director. (Important matters which will have considerable effect on the company are always referred to the board of directors.) When you attend the annual meeting and vote on the issuing, buying, or selling of shares or substantial assets, you are a shareholder. The shareholder always has the final say on any serious issue because shareholdings represent ownership of the company.

The minor shareholder who holds less than 50% of the issued shares is usually in a precarious position in relation to the major shareholder who holds more than 50% of the issued shares. If you are involved in a two-person corporation where the parties are not related (i.e., it is not a family company), the parties should divide the shares equally. If this cannot be done, competent legal advice should be obtained by at least the minority shareholder. If there are substantial assets involved, both parties should seek professional advice.

You might ask what will happen when there is a basic disagreement over some issue and a deadlock results. The answer is that either the assets are sold and the business wound up or one party buys out the other. We all know what happens when partners in a business have an irreconcilable difference. The same is true in a close corporation.

Another advantage of the equal share split is that it encourages cooperation. When this balance is altered it will, of necessity, affect the personal relationship of the partners.

6. One-person corporations

Oregon law ORS 57.306 allows the formation of one-person corporations. This means that the same person may be the sole director, sole shareholder, and sole officer (i.e., president and secretary).

The evolution of one-person corporations recognizes the fact that many people are in business solely with and for themselves. Rather than having a "nominal" second shareholder who performs no real function and serves no purpose, it was considered desirable to allow a single person to obtain the advantages of incorporation.

The procedures for incorporating a one-person corporation are the same as those for incorporating any close corporation, and the required annual meetings can be held with only one person in attendance.

7. Classes of shares

Shares can have an infinite number of restrictions or rights attached to them. Some of the more common types are "common," "preferred" (as to dividends, right to share in assets in the event of liquidation, etc.), "redeemable cumulative," and "voting."

In the vast majority of new close corporations, it is not necessary at the outset to place special rights and restrictions on your issued shares. Later, if you feel that there is a need for a more complicated share structure, you can seek competent legal advice in order to carry out the alterations correctly and to design your capital structure in order to maximize tax and control advantages.

It is recommended that all shares be simply "common" which gives each shareholder equal rights in voting, dividends, etc. Furthermore, unless you receive sound advice on the matter, and know what you are doing, it is wise to avoid starting off with different classes of shares. Only those small business corporations with common shares can take advantage of the sometimes favorable tax treatment offered by the subchapter S and section 1244 provisions of the Internal Revenue Code. A corporation whose shares give all shareholders the same rights has "common" shares.

8. Kinds of shares

Oregon has eliminated the concept of "par value." Historically, par value was the share price fixed by the board of directors. The shares of stock could not be issued from treasury for less than the set amount. Shares with no par value could be issued for any amount. The distinction between par and no par value had little real significance because immediately after either was issued, its value rose or fell depending on its true market value.

3

TAX ADVANTAGES TO INCORPORATING

a. INTRODUCTION

If your business made $50,000 last year as a proprietorship, the entire amount would be taxed at your personal income tax rate. If you have incorporated, $25,000 could be paid to you personally and $25,000 left in the corporation. Individual tax rates are different from corporate rates. The IRS allows you to work almost any combination that keeps your total tax bill to a minimum.

Note: If you expect your business to either lose money, break even or make a small profit, please refer to the discussion of subchapter S and section 1244 elections.

A corporation allows you to increase significantly the amount of compensation put away in retirement (deferred) plans for the benefit of yourself and your family. (See page 18 for further details.)

You can also effect substantial estate planning advantages. As this is a technical area and beyond the scope of this book, this advantage will not be discussed at any length. The existence of a corporation enables you to own a widely diversified portfolio of assets (including all kinds of property) under the ownership of a single entity. This can be a great advantage both from a tax and an administrative point of view.

b. TAX PLANS AVAILABLE TO CORPORATIONS ONLY

1. Subchapter S corporations

When a corporation earns profits, it must pay a federal income tax on those profits. If the profits are distributed as dividends to shareholders, the shareholders must report the dividends as ordinary income and pay an income tax on the dividends. This results in *double taxation of the same funds*. This double taxation can be avoided if you take a salary equal to the amount of the profit, which in effect reduces the corporation profit to zero. (Then there is no corporate tax.) This can be a tax advantage if the earnings are substantial. However, for most new businesses the profit is very meager for the first few years.

For this reason Congress has enacted Internal Revenue Code Sections 1371 to 1379, commonly known as "subchapter S," which provides the means to avoid this double taxation. Under subchapter S, the corporation *is not required* to pay any federal income tax on its profits. Subchapter S permits the corporation to pay the profits, or dividends, directly to the individual shareholders who would then report the income as ordinary income and pay an income tax. This eliminates the double income tax on the same funds. Losses are also passed on to the shareholders.

The primary aim of subchapter S is to encourage the incorporation of small businesses and to allow certain advantages to small business corporations in an effort to ensure their success in the initial stages of operation. Under the subchapter S election, corporate income is, in effect, taxed at the individual rates rather than the corporate rate. Remember, this is advantageous only when corporate income is small. After the operation becomes a success and begins to generate large taxable income, the shareholders may want to terminate the election in order to take advantage of the lower corporate tax rate.

(a) Eligibility to elect under subchapter S

To make an election under subchapter S a corporation must be a "small business corporation" meeting the following conditions:

(i) Shareholders: A subchapter S corporation must not have more than 35 shareholders.

(ii) Individual shareholder (estates and some trusts) only: All stock must be owned by individuals, estates, and certain trusts including a trust created primarily to exercise voting power of stock transferred to it. A corporation is ineligible for subchapter S election if its stock is owned by another corporation, a partnership or a nonqualified trust.

(iii) One class of stock: The electing corporation may not have more than one class of stock. The term "class of stock" is not defined by the statute; however, the regulations state that if the outstanding shares "are not identical with respect to the rights and interests which they convey in the control, profits and assets of the corporation," the corporation is considered to have more than one class of stock. In other words, all shares must be common shares.

(iv) Nonresident alien shareholders: The corporation may not have any nonresident alien shareholders. This restriction reflects the fact that the corporate income is excepted from tax under subchapter S on the assumption that it will be subject to the graduated individual income tax rates, whereas some nonresident aliens are taxed at a flat rate of 30%.

(v) Membership in an "affiliated group" under section 1504: The corporation may not elect under subchapter S if it is a member of an "affiliated group" defined by § 1501, relating to consolidated returns.

(vi) Election: Rules governing the time and method of making the election in its effective date are prescribed by § 1372. The election is made by the corporation, but all shareholders must consent. The election is made on Form 2553, which is filed together with the consents of all shareholders. It is filed with the Internal Revenue officer designated in the form instructions. You have to be certain that the form is filed on time and you should in all cases keep a copy with a stamp from the IRS with the date and the time they received the election. This will prevent any future problems should the election form be lost.

The general rule on the time for making the election is as follows: the election must be filed for any taxable year *either* on or before the 15th day of the third month of the current tax year or at any time during the preceding tax year. Therefore, a calendar year corporation would make elections either by March 15 of the taxable year or any time in the preceding tax year.

There seems to be no authority for the grant by the IRS of an extension of time to file an election. However, an extension may be granted for filing the shareholder consents. In no event should an election be deferred because some of the required consents cannot be obtained in time. In order for an election to be valid it must be filed on time, otherwise it will be ineffective not only for the current taxable year but also for all succeeding taxable years.

You will see that in the example of Form 2553 (Sample #3), the shareholders have consented. A new shareholder does not have to file a consent in order for the corporation to maintain its subchapter S status.

In addition, the board of directors should draw up minutes of a meeting or consent resolutions in lieu of a meeting, in which the subchapter S election is discussed and adopted. For example, the resolutions in Sample #4 would be inserted into the Minutes of the Organizational Meeting of Directors of a new corporation if the directors decided to make the subchapter S election.

(b) Termination of subchapter S election

Once an election is made under subchapter S it is effective for the taxable year of the corporation and for all succeeding taxable years unless it is terminated in one of the following ways:

(i) Revocation: It can be terminated by majority of stockholders, effective on date of revocation or a date in the future.

(ii) Disqualification: The election is terminated if the corporation ceases to be a "small business corporation." In other words, if more holders than allowable acquire stock, or a nonresident alien shareholder who is not an individual, estate or qualified trust acquires stock, or if more than one class of stock is issued, then the corporation will be disqualified for subchapter S status.

(iii) Passive investment income: The election terminates if more than 25% of the corporation's gross receipts constitute "passive investment income" for each of three consecutive tax years. Passive investment income includes gross receipts from royalties, rents, dividends, interest and annuities and gain from the sale or exchange of stock or securities. The purpose of this limitation is to restrict the use of subchapter S to corporations having substantial amounts of operating income as opposed to investment income. The restraint is not applied to an electing corporation for the first or second taxable year of active conduct of a trade or business if its passive income is less than $3,000. This protects the election for a corporation in its initial years if, for example, its principal source of gross receipts is interest on bank accounts because normal operations have not properly commenced.

It should be noted that the 20% restriction on passive income refers to the corporation's "gross receipts" rather than its "gross income" apparently to facilitate use of the subchapter S election by corporations operating at a loss, which might be disqualified by the 20% requirement if gross income were the relevant standard.

Publication #589 is available from the IRS to help provide tax information on subchapter S corporations.

2. Section 1244 benefits

Section 1244 of the Internal Revenue Code permits shareholders to adopt a stock plan where shareholders can claim an ordinary loss treatment of their lost investment if the venture fails. This section is aimed at encouraging the investment of capital in small corporate ventures. The result is better than capital tax loss treatment. In other words, the corporation can protect its shareholders by preparing in advance for the consequences of the corporation's failure.

This may be accomplished by the corporation electing to qualify its shares as *Internal Revenue Code section 1244* stock. To qualify its shares under *Internal Revenue Code section 1244*, the corporation must meet the following requirements:

(a) The shareholders must be individuals and not corporations or trusts, although partnerships can qualify under special rules.

(b) The board of directors must elect to qualify the corporation stock as *section 1244 stock, in writing.* (See Sample #17 in chapter 6.)

When the corporation's stock has been qualified as section 1244 stock, the shareholder can take a *100% ordinary tax*

SAMPLE #3
ELECTION BY A SMALL BUSINESS CORPORATION

Form **2553** Department of the Treasury Internal Revenue Service

Election by a Small Business Corporation
(As to taxable status under subchapter S of the Internal Revenue Code)

File in duplicate

NOTE.—This election under section 1372(a) (with the consent of all your stockholders) to be treated as an "electing small business corporation" for income tax purposes may be made only if the corporation meets all six of the requirements stated in instruction A.

Name of corporation	Employer identification number (see instr. L)	Principal business activity (see instr. E)
P & P Industries		Printing

Number and street	Election is to be effective for the taxable year beginning (Mo., day, year)
1000 A Street	March 1, 199-
City or town, State and ZIP code	**Number of shares issued and outstanding**
Yourtown, Oregon 97000	250
Is the corporation the outgrowth or continuation of any form of predecessor? ☐ Yes ☒ No. If "Yes," state name of predecessor, type of organization, and period during which it was in existence.	Date and place of incorporation March 1, 199- Yourtown, Oregon

If this election is effective for the first taxable year the corporation is in existence, submit the following information:

Date corporation first had shareholders	Date corporation first had assets	Date corporation began doing business	Annual return will be filed for taxable year ending (Month)
March 10, 199-	March 10, 199-	March 15, 199-	March, 199-

Name and address (including ZIP code) of each shareholder	Stock: No. of shares	Stock: Date(s) acquired (see instr. D)	Social Security Number	Internal Revenue Service Center where individual return is filed
1. Jack Printer, 1000 A Street Yourtown, Oregon 97000	125	March 10 199-	021-11-0123	Ogden, Utah
2. Jane Printer, 1000 A Street Yourtown, Oregon 97000	125	March 10 199-	012-22-3201	Ogden, Utah
3.				
4.				
5.				
6.				
7.				
8.				
9.				
10.				

NOTE.—For this election to be valid, the consent of each stockholder must accompany this form or be shown below. See instruction D.

Under penalties of perjury, I declare that I have examined this election, including accompanying schedules and statements, and to the best of my knowledge and belief it is true, correct, and complete.

Signature and Title of Officer ➧ Jack Printer President Date March 30, 199-

Shareholders' statement of consent (May be used in lieu of attachments—see instruction D)

We the undersigned shareholders consent to the election of the above corporation to be treated as an "electing small business corporation" under section 1372(a).

Signature of shareholders and date

1	Jack Printer	6	
2	Jane Printer	7	
3		8	
4		9	
5		10	

(Send both copies to the Internal Revenue Service.)

SAMPLE #4
SUBCHAPTER S RESOLUTIONS

The president suggested that the corporation consider electing to be taxed as a small business corporation under Internal Revenue Code subchapter S. The board then discussed the advantages of such an action and on motion, the following resolutions were adopted:

RESOLVED, that the corporation elects to be taxed under Internal Revenue Code subchapter S as a small business corporation;

RESOLVED FURTHER, that the officers of the corporation are authorized and directed to prepare, execute and file, or cause to be prepared, executed and filed, Internal Revenue Service Form 2553, together with a statement by each shareholder consenting to this election, and to do all other acts that may be required to make this election effective.

loss rather than a 50% capital loss if the following conditions are met:

(a) The stock became worthless within two years from the date of the election when the board of directors voted to qualify the stock as section 1244 stock.

(b) The shareholder owned and held stock for more than six months prior to the date it was deemed to have become worthless.

(c) The shareholders purchased the stock from the corporation only and not from other shareholders.

(d) The stock is *common* stock issued by a domestic corporation.

(e) The limits on how much stock may be sold under this plan are complied with (ordinarily this does not concern the average small business).

3. Employee benefit plans

Deferred compensation (a pension) represents one of the best forms of tax shelter for a person who owns a controlling interest in a profitable, closely held corporation. Unlike oil drilling programs and other risky enterprises, the advantages of employee benefit plans include not only the immediate tax benefit but also may result in conservation and growth of capital in a tax sheltered investment program.

Qualified plans provide the corporate employer and its employees with substantial tax advantages which include:

(a) Contributions to deferred compensation plans within certain limits are tax deductible by the employer.

(b) Benefits received by an employee are taxed only upon their receipt (usually at retirement when the employee is in a lower tax bracket) and are often subject to favorable tax treatment at that time.

(c) Earnings from a trust established to fund the plan, its earnings are exempt from income tax. The income is taxed when the participant employee receives it, and often favorable tax rates or special averaging provisions apply.

(d) Death benefits, payable to anyone other than the deceased employee's estate which arise from an employer's contributions to a qualified plan are not included in the employee's gross estate for federal estate tax purposes and are also exempt from Oregon state inheritance taxes. Moreover, tax exempt status under estate and inheritance tax laws continues in the case of certain retirement annuity contracts purchased at retirement for the employee participant in deferred compensation plans.

(e) The corporate employer is able to reduce its earnings and profit by its contribution to a qualified plan of deferred compensation. This helps to avoid accumulated earnings tax problems and reduce exposure to dividend tax treatment.

(f) Funds contributed to a separate employee benefit plan trust may help the corporate employer to decrease the net worth of the business and thereby reduce the value of its stock for gift and estate tax purposes.

(g) Corporations may also establish medical reimbursement plans for employees, their spouses, and their children, thereby having the corporation pay their medical expenses with tax deductible dollars.

Qualified plans should be an important consideration, particularly in the case of small, closely held family corporations. These advantages become most important when the business is prospering and the controlling shareholders are thinking about estate planning.

4

GOOD BUSINESS PRACTICES

a. YOU AND YOUR BOOKS

The first motto of a small corporation or small business should be, "Do not dread bookkeeping." It is an integral part of your business which records, summarizes and analyzes your financial activity.

You do not need books "just because the IRS tells you to keep books." You need a well-kept set of books because accurate, up-to-date information helps you make the best business decisions possible. You cannot keep all aspects of your business in your head. The total financial picture should be there for you to look at, especially where personal and corporate finances can mingle and become confused.

If you are involved in a retail business, or even providing services, you have to know how much your fixed costs, such as rent, utilities, taxes, supplies, and insurance, are costing you every day you open for business. Then you know what to charge, as you have a more complete idea of what it is costing you to sell.

As you will read in "Post-incorporation procedures" (see chapter 7), you must open a bank account in your corporate name. Some small business advisors suggest that it is easier to keep track of your business money by —

(a) paying all bills by check (or as many as possible),

(b) depositing all business income in the corporate account,

(c) withdrawing all personal use money first, as a withdrawal or a personal draw, and then using the money to pay for personal items.

In other words, never make use of the corporate money directly to pay for a personal item. Months later you won't remember what or who it was for. Furthermore, it will complicate your income tax calculation.

It is often a good idea to have an accountant or competent bookkeeper come in and train either an employee or yourself in how to properly keep useable business records.

b. THE USE OF FINANCIAL STATEMENTS

No matter what legal form an organization may take, the preparation of meaningful financial statements is vital. This is because various people will have an interest in the financial affairs of the organization, namely owners, managers, creditors, the Internal Revenue Service, the state of Oregon and prospective buyers.

To illustrate, assume that you are a bank manager and that J & J Personnel Inc., a medium-sized corporation in the employment agency business, approaches you for a $10,000 loan. The principals explain that the funds are necessary for office expansion. As a prospective creditor you would be interested in two things: the ability of J & J Personnel Inc. to pay the regular instalments of principal and interest on the loan and the amount you, the bank, would recover if the corporation could not meet its obligation. To satisfy your curiosity in this regard, you would have to examine the financial statements of the corporation. The annual income would be shown on the profit and loss statement. This figure, if compared with the income from prior periods, would indicate to you the rate of economic growth of the enterprise.

In addition you would be able to determine whether or not enough total revenue is generated to repay the proposed loan. The balance sheet of the corporation would indicate any other long-term debt for which the corporation is liable. Furthermore, you would be able to determine which assets (inventories, accounts receivable, etc.) are available as security for the proposed loan.

The corporation's ability to pay its current obligations is another important indicator of the economic health of the enterprise. This ability to pay present debts when due can also be determined from the balance sheet. This indicator is expressed as a ratio (called the "current ratio") and is calculated by subtracting the total of the current liabilities from the total current assets. This part is illustrated in the very simple example in Sample #5.

Current assets exceed current liabilities in the ratio of 2:1. In other words, the working capital position of the corporation in this case is healthy.

You would obtain much of the information so vital to your decision regarding the loan by looking at the financial statements of J & J Personnel Inc.

The preceding illustration showed how financial statements can be useful to potential creditors. Financial statements are useful to anyone who has an interest (monetary or otherwise) in an enterprise. Just as certain medical implements are the tools by which a doctor can get some indication of physical health, so financial statements are the tools by which interested parties can measure the economic health of an organization.

Following is a breakdown in point form of the three major financial statements: the balance sheet, the profit and loss statement and the earned surplus statement. They are discussed here to give you some idea of the function and contents of financial statements.

1. The balance sheet

The balance sheet is a positive statement, not an historical record, and shows what is owned and owed at a given date.

There are three sections to a balance sheet: assets, liabilities, and owners' equity.

(a) Assets

Current assets are those assets which will be used up within one year of the current balance sheet date. Normal valuation of such assets is at original cost or market value, whichever is the lower.

Fixed assets are those assets that will provide benefits to the organization over a longer period than one year from the current balance sheet date. Valuation is generally at original cost less accumulated depreciation. The amount of depreciation is based on the length of the useful life of the asset and the original cost of the asset.

To illustrate:

Building: original cost $20,000
Useful life: 10 years

Portion of asset cost which expires in each period:

$$\frac{\$20,000}{10} = \$2,000$$

SAMPLE #5
BALANCE SHEET
(Partial)

J & J PERSONNEL INC.
MARCH 31, 199-

CURRENT ASSETS		CURRENT LIABILITIES	
Cash	$ 20,000	Trade payables	$100,000
Accounts receivable	290,000	Wages payable	10,000
Inventories	90,000	Current portion of long-term debt	90,000
TOTAL	**$400,000**	**TOTAL**	**$200,000**

This type of depreciation can be calculated on a reducing balance basis, but the following is an example of the straight-line method. The sum of $2,000 is charged to the profit and loss statement in each period and is accumulated on the balance sheet as a reduction of the original cost of the asset. Five years after the building was purchased, the balance sheet would show:

Building, at cost	$20,000
Less accumulated depreciation (5 x $2,000)	10,000
Book value of building	$10,000

Because the asset may be sold for more than the original cost, the book value does not necessarily indicate the amount the equity-holders should receive for their ownership of the building. (**Note**: the "equity-holders" in a corporation are the shareholders.)

(b) Liabilities and owners' equity

The nature of these items becomes evident in the illustration of a typical balance sheet shown in Sample #6.

2. Profit and loss statement

This statement indicates the profit or loss by subtracting the total expenses of a period from the total revenue for that period. There are two ways of determining when revenue is earned and when expenses are incurred: cash basis and accrual basis.

On cash basis, no revenue is recognized until cash is received. No expenses are recognized until cash is paid out. On accrual basis, revenue is recognized as soon as it is earned. Expenses are recognized as soon as they are incurred. The date cash is received or paid out is irrelevant.

3. Earned surplus statement

This statement shows what happens to net profit. The last figure on a balance sheet represents earned surplus. This is the part of previous earnings that is retained by the corporation after providing for reserves and paying all operating expenses, accrued interest (on long-term loans), income taxes, and dividends. The earned surplus belongs to the shareholders, but it is retained in the operation as a cushion to absorb possible losses, to protect the corporation from any other unforeseen occurrences, and to be a part of the capital of the operation.

c. YOU AND YOUR EMPLOYEES

Before you hire an employee you should be aware that each employee will just about double your paper work. All employers must keep separate payroll records for each employee; withhold federal income tax, social security taxes, state income, and possibly state disability taxes; calculate quarterly and year-end payroll tax returns, the employer's portion of social security taxes and unemployment taxes; purchase workers' compensation insurance; and prepare year-end earnings statements for each employee. Some people have estimated that the paper work involved and the necessary payments cost an additional 30% of the payroll. Therefore, if you pay an employee $3.00 per hour it is really costing you approximately $3.90 per hour by the time you pay for all of the accompanying services.

In addition, there is no leeway or gray area given by the federal government or state governments in the area of payroll taxes. Your business could be locked up and bank account impounded if you are even a few weeks late with your payroll tax returns.

Therefore, you should think it over carefully before deciding to hire a large number of employees. Basically, if you can hire what the IRS considers independent contractors, you might save yourself a lot of trouble. An independent contractor is someone who is in business for himself or herself and differs from an employee in that the services he or she offers is to the public at large (and not limited to a single employer). Independent contractors have control over the

SAMPLE #6
BALANCE SHEET OF AN UNINCORPORATED BUSINESS

XYZ GROCERY
(Not Incorporated)
November 20, 199-

		ASSETS	
Current assets			
Cash on hand and in bank		720.12	
Accounts receivable less allowance for doubtful accounts		657.72	
Merchandise inventory valued at the lower of original cost or market		3,212.63	
Prepaid expenses		157.55	
Total current assets			$4,748.02
Fixed assets — at cost			
Land		2,320.00	
Building	$5,767.16		
Less: accumulated depreciation	1,727.92	4,039.24	
Store fixtures	3,726.12		
Less: accumulated depreciation	982.36	2,743.76	
Delivery truck	2,760.20		
Less: accumulated depreciation	513.60	2,246.60	11,349.60
			16,097.62
	LIABILITIES & PARTNERS' EQUITY		
Current liabilities			
Trade accounts payable		$2,772.18	
Accrued wages		75.20	
Employees' income tax payable		60.16	
Accrued real estate taxes		220.00	
Total current liabilities			3,127.54
Earned surplus of partners' equity*			
Jones' share		$6,484.84	
Smith's share		$6,484.85	
			12,969.69
			$16,097.23

*If incorporated this would read as follows:

CAPITAL STOCK
Common stock, no par value, maximum selling price $1
Authorized — 10,000 shares
Issued and fully paid for:
Jones — 50 shares at $0.01 = $0.50
Smith — 50 shares at $0.01 = $0.50

Retained earnings **$12,969.69**

You will note that Jones and Smith still have equity of a total of **$12,969.69**

method and results of the services they provide, and they determine when and how it shall be done. For example, you could hire a part-time person to come in and clean the office and provide him or her with the necessary mops, brooms, and wash pails. On the other hand, you could avoid a lot of paper work and payroll taxes by hiring a cleaning company to come in with their own equipment and clean the offices according to your instructions. A doctor or dentist might hire an office services company to look after the filing, reservations, and supplies, rather than hiring an employee to do the same thing.

I must stress that it is very important that you carefully consider the legal status of all those who do work for you. Even if you do not call a person an employee, he or she *is* an employee if IRS considers him or her to be one.

In any event you will find the IRS publication *Tax Guide for Small Business* (Publication #334) of great assistance if you are considering becoming an employer. It is wise to get your identification process underway with the IRS and state agencies before you actually hire anyone, because of the initial amount of paper work.

You should note that if you do decide to hire an independent contractor, the only form you are responsible for is Form 1099 — Misc. which must be filed for every outside contractor to whom you paid more than $600 during the year.

5

HOW MANY SHARES TO ISSUE

A common question that arises about shares is, "Why not issue all the shares at the beginning?" The main reason for this is primarily taxation.

Every business needs capital to begin operations. Capital flows into business two ways:

(a) By investing in shares, i.e., equity capital

(b) By lending money to the business in some form or other, e.g., shareholder loans, bonds, debentures.

There are definite advantages to establishing the capital of a business through loans instead of issuing stock, especially in a high-risk business such as a newly-incorporated partnership or proprietorship.

The first advantage is that capital "loaned" to the corporation, as opposed to "invested" in the corporation, can be repaid at any time tax-free, i.e., a loan to the corporation repaid to a shareholder is not income to the shareholder. On the other hand, money invested in shares cannot be repaid while the corporation is operating. Therefore, any withdrawal of capital by the owners must be done through payment of dividends which are taxable to the corporation and its shareholders unless a subchapter S election is made. Capital invested in shares can be recovered tax-free only when the corporation is wound up and its capital distributed.

Second, if the new corporation is near financial collapse, a shareholder loan ranks equally with the other creditors when dividing up the remainder of the assets and ahead of repayment to the shareholders for money invested in shares. Common shareholders rarely see any proceeds when a corporation goes bankrupt.

However, care must be taken in determining a proper ratio. If too much is "loaned" the IRS may declare the capital to be an investment, thereby making any repayment a dividend.

Another reason for not issuing all the shares is that they have to be paid for at the time they are issued out of the treasury. There is no good reason to put a large amount of capital from share purchases into the corporation treasury. There is usually little advantage in financing the corporation by large investments from shareholders.

If all the shares are issued immediately after incorporation and if a new shareholder wishes to join existing shareholders without obtaining their shares, then an amendment to the articles must be filed in order to increase the amount of authorized capital. The procedure for amending your articles is explained in chapter 12, and it is not very difficult. Nevertheless, a little thought before you divide up the total amount of authorized capital can save some time and effort later.

A final and most important reason not to issue all shares is that if your corporation is successful, you may wish to bring in other "partners" to invest in the business. At that time, valuation of the amount of "equity" you have in the business will have to be made by your accountant. Equity is defined as assets minus liabilities and represents the net worth of the business. Samples #7 and #8 illustrate that it makes no difference how many total shares are issued as long as your position in relation to the other shareholders is not altered. Also, by keeping most of the shares in the treasury, you will be flexible enough to meet new corporate developments.

SAMPLE #7
BALANCE SHEET
(100 shares issued)

J & J PERSONNEL INCORPORATED

ASSETS	
Cash	$1,000
Inventory	4,000
Building	5,000
TOTAL ASSETS	**$10,000**
LIABILITIES	
Note to the bank	$2,000
Shareholder loan	3,000
TOTAL LIABILITIES	**$5,000**
NET WORTH	
Capital stock authorized — 50,000 shares	
Issued 100 shares at $5 each	$500
50 to A for $250	
50 to B for $250	
Retained earnings	$4,500
TOTAL EQUITY	**$5,000**
TOTAL LIABILITIES AND EQUITY	**$10,000**

NOTE: A and B each have shares worth (in hard cash) $250, or a total of $500. But since $500 of the $5,000 equity is their own money the net gain for each is $2,250 (1/2 x 4,500).

SAMPLE #8
BALANCE SHEET
(50,000 shares issued)

J & J PERSONNEL INCORPORATED

ASSETS	
Cash	$50,500
Inventory	4,000
Building	5,000
TOTAL ASSETS	**$59,500**
LIABILITIES	
Note to the bank	$2,000
Shareholder loan	3,000
TOTAL LIABILITIES	**$5,000**
NET WORTH	
Capital stock authorized — 50,000 shares	
Issued 50,000 shares at $1 each 25,000 to A for $25,000 and 25,000 to B for $25,000	$50,000
Earned surplus	$4,500
TOTAL EQUITY	**$54,500**
TOTAL LIABILITIES AND EQUITY	**$59,500**

NOTE: If the business is wound up, both A's and B's shares are worth $54,500, but as $50,000 is their own money, the net gain is $2,250 (1/2 x 4,500), the same as in Sample #7.

Think of all the shares that are not issued as being in a large pot with the label "corporate treasury." While they stay in that pot they belong to the corporation. Just because you incorporate with 10,000 shares does not mean that all the shares have to be issued to people. The shares can belong to the corporation for any length of time. You, as a director, may issue more shares to existing shareholders or to a new shareholder from the supply available in the pot.

Shareholders' contributions are not included in the balance sheet as this is like transferring money from one hand to the other. Similarly, "good will" has been ignored in both examples.

Another common situation is where a third shareholder is brought in. In such a case you have two alternatives to consider. First, you may simply transfer a percentage of each of the existing shareholders' holdings to the new "partner." If the shares are sold for more than you paid for them, you will have to think about the capital gains tax liability.

Another problem with this method is that frequently you end up with a fractional share situation which is always annoying. For example, in our model company we have John and Jack Doe each owning 50 shares. Say their cousin Hilda becomes involved and all parties agree that she should be an equal shareholder. In order to do this, both Jack and John would have to transfer 16-2/3 shares to Hilda and each party would be left with 33-1/3 — an awkward situation. A better solution would be to issue 25 more shares each to John and Jack Doe and then transfer them to Hilda. Again, taxes would have to be considered if the shares are transferred at a higher price than they were issued for. If, on the other hand, the shares were issued at, say, $5 per share, this amount was paid into the corporation, and the shares then transferred for the same amount, then no tax would be payable.

In the second case, the additional shares could be issued directly from the treasury to Hilda at the price agreed on, and no tax would be payable because the money simply flows into the capital account of the corporation. Of course, there would also be no direct benefit to John and Jack in bringing Hilda in, other than for her contribution to the work effort. In other words, the corporation would have additional funds with which to finance its activities, but Jack and John could not receive any financial benefit from Hilda's purchase without paying tax.

In most cases, then, it is simpler to issue additional shares, either directly to the new shareholder, or to the existing members first and then transfer them to the new partner, rather than to get involved in complicated partial share arrangements.

To recap briefly, since there is no particular advantage to issuing all the shares unless you are involved in a complicated share control problem, and several disadvantages to capitalizing through share capital, it is wise to issue a minimum to begin with, say 50 to 100, depending on the number of persons involved.

6

INCORPORATION PROCEDURE IN OREGON

a. PRELIMINARY MATTERS

Every person proposing to incorporate should have a copy of the Oregon Business Corporation Act, chapter 57. It is clearly written and well indexed and organized. You can get a free copy by writing or phoning:

Corporation Commissioner
Commerce Building
158 12th Street N.E.
Salem, Oregon 97310-0210
Telephone: 378-4166

Following is a general, abbreviated, step-by-step description of the procedures necessary to incorporate a private company in Oregon. (For a complete checklist, refer to the Appendix.)

b. CHOOSING YOUR CORPORATE NAME

As with all persons, a corporation must have a name. There are certain factors that must be considered in choosing this name, the most important being that a corporation name cannot be used without the Corporation Commissioner's approval.

The following is a reprint of sections of the Oregon Business Corporation Act which outline the guidelines used for acceptable corporate names.

57.045 Corporate name. (1) The corporate name:

(a) Shall contain the word "corporation," "company," "incorporated" or "limited," or shall contain an abbreviation of one of such words.

(b) Shall not contain any word or phrase which indicates or implies that it is organized for any purpose other than one or more of the purposes contained in its articles of incorporation.

(c) Shall not be the same as, or deceptively similar to, any other corporate, limited partnership, reserved or registered name currently on file with the Corporation Commissioner, the Insurance Commissioner or the Superintendent of Banks, an assumed business name registered as provided in ORS 648.010 or a trade-mark, trade name or service mark registered as provided in ORS chapter 647, except that this provision shall not apply if the applicant files with the Corporation Commissioner either of the following:

(A) The written consent of such other corporation or holder of a reserved or registered name to use the same or deceptively similar name and one or more words are added to make such name distinguishable from such other name; or

(B) A certified copy of a final decree of a court of competent jurisdiction establshing the prior right of the applicant to the use of such name in this state.

(2) Nothing contained in this section shall preclude a corporation from transacting business under an assumed business name.

Here are a number of simple checks that increase your chances of picking an acceptable name:

(a) Use the yellow pages of your nearest metropolitan phone book to check names of existing corporations in your field.

(b) Check trade and corporation directories to see that no one else has used that exact name.

(c) A coined word, plus a term descriptive of the major activity of the business, has the best chance of success. Thus, if Bill Scott and Jack Jones are starting a transmission repair business, a name such as "Bill-Jack Transmission Inc." is likely to be approved.

You can find out if any other business is registered under the name you want by calling the office of the Corporation Commissioner at 378-4166.

To reserve a name, you must send a letter (see Sample #9) together with $5 to the Corporation Commissioner. You cannot reserve a name over the phone. If the Corporation Commissioner finds that the name is available, it will be reserved for you for 120 days. This can be extended for another 120 days by repeating the procedure.

SAMPLE #9
LETTER FOR RESERVATION OF CORPORATE NAME

November 1, 199-

Corporation Commissioner
Commerce Building
158 12th Street N.E.
Salem, Oregon 97310-0210

Dear Corporation Commissioner:

This is to request that you reserve the name

Bill-Jack Transmission Inc.

for the corporation that Bill Scott and Jack Jones intend to organize. It is to be a transmission repair business. The name is derived from the two first names of the incorporators. Enclosed is a check for $5 to reserve the name for 120 days.

Sincerely, *Bill Scott*

Bill Scott

Jack Jones.

Jack Jones

c. THE ARTICLES OF INCORPORATION

The information required to be in the Articles of Incorporation is specified in ORS 57.311. The basic forms necessary to incorporate in the state of Oregon are shown on the following pages. Included is a sample of the Articles of Incorporation (see Sample #10). Standard form articles are available from the publisher or where you bought this book. See Table #1 for filing fees.

The articles state the capitalization of the corporation including the aggregate number of shares which the corporation shall have the authority to issue and, if there are various classes of stock, the number of shares of each class. If the shares are divided into classes or issued in series, a statement of the relative rights, preferences, and limitations applying to each of the classes must be made on the articles. Keep in mind that the taxation benefits of subchapter S and section 1244 are not available to closely held small corporations if they have different classes of shares.

The issue of corporate control becomes more complicated when different classes of shares exist. If you plan to incorporate with different classes of shares you would be wise to consult an attorney to set up the different rights and to make sure you understand how the division of rights will affect the operation of the corporation.

1. Preparing the Articles

(a) Article 1

The name of the corporation must contain the words "Corporation," "Company," "Incorporated," or "Limited," or an abbreviation of one of these words. The duration is presumed to be perpetual unless otherwise stated.

(b) Article 2

There is no limit on the number of shares the corporation can issue. As discussed in chapter 5, do *not* issue all of the shares.

(c) Article 3

The address of the registered office and the name of the registered agent at this address must be stated here. The registered office and the registered agent provide an identifiable place and person where legal documents may be served and to which the Corporation Commissioner's office may forward materials of concern to the corporation. This means that a street address, not a post office box number, must be given. It can, however, be a residence address. See Sample #37 for a change of registered agent and/or office.

(d) Article 4

You may direct notices from the Corporation Division be sent to an address different from that of the registered agent.

(e) Article 5

State the name and address of each incorporator. One person will normally be the incorporator. Each incorporator must sign the Articles of Incorporation.

(f) Article 6

State the name and address of each director. (This step is optional.)

(g) Article 7

Aside from the statute (ORS Chapt. 57), the Articles of Incorporation and the by-laws will control corporate activities. If there are any important restrictions or limitations on corporate activities and affairs they should be stated in this article; generally, restrictions or optional provisions are not advisable unless a specific purpose is being served.

2. Filing the articles

Duplicate originals of the Articles of Incorporation must be filed with the Corporation Commissioner along with the fees.

The filing fee and the annual license fees must be paid in the first year and sent with your Articles of Incorporation. See Table #1 for filing and license fees.

Note: Fees are subject to change. You may obtain the most recent fee schedule by contacting the Corporation Division at (503) 378-4166.

Send a letter to the Corporation Commissioner, enclosing the documents. The letter in Sample #11 is the suggested form.

When you have completed everything correctly, the Corporation Commissioner will file one copy of your articles and issue a "Certificate of Incorporation" to which is attached the second original; it is returned to you for the corporate files. Insert this in your minute book. Although at one time the certificate of incorporation was an actual "certificate," it is now a computer printout.

SAMPLE #10
ARTICLES OF INCORPORATION

Submit the original
and one true copy
$50.00

ARTICLES OF INCORPORATION

Registry Number: ____________

Business Corporation

PLEASE TYPE OR PRINT LEGIBLY IN BLACK INK

ARTICLE 1: Name of the corporation: J & J Personnel Inc.
Note: The name must contain the word "Corporation," "Company," "Incorporated," or "Limited," or one of such words.

ARTICLE 2: Number of shares the coporation will have the authority to issue: 1,000

ARTICLE 3: Name of the initial registered agent: Jay Pumpkin

Address of initial registered office (must be a **street** address in Oregon which is identical to the registered agent's business office):

123 First Street — Anytown — Oregon — 00000
Street and number — City — Zip code

Mailing address of registered agent (if different from the registered office):

Oregon
Street and number or PO box — City — Zip code

ARTICLE 4: Address where the Division may mail notices: (Attn:) Jack Pumpkin

P.O. Box 007 — Anytown — Oregon — 00000
Street and number or PO box — City — State — Zip code

ARTICLE 5: Name and address of each incorporator:

Jay Pumpkin, 123 First Street, Anytown, OR

ARTICLE 6: Name and address of each director: (optional)

ARTICLE 7: Other optional provisions (Attach additional sheets, if necessary)

Execution:

Jay Pumpkin — Jay Pumpkin — Incorporator
Signature — Printed name — Title

Jack Pumpkin — Jack Pumpkin — Incorporator
Signature — Printed name — Title

Please make checks payable to the Corporation Division. Submit the completed form and fee to: Corporation Division, Business Registry, 158 12th Street NE, Salem, Oregon 97310-0210

SAMPLE #11
LETTER TO CORPORATE COMMISSIONER

Corporation Commissioner
Commerce Building
158 12th Street NE
Salem, Oregon 97310-0210

Dear Corporation Commissioner:

Re: Incorporation of J & J Personnel Inc.

Enclosed herewith are the following documents:

1. Two executed* originals of the Articles of Incorporation
2. Our check in the amount of $_____ payable to the Corporation Commissioner to cover your fees.

Would you kindly attend to the incorporation of the above-mentioned company and return a certified copy of the articles as soon as possible.

Yours truly,

John Doe

*"Executed" means signed and notarized.

TABLE #1
FEE SCHEDULE*

ASSUMED BUSINESS NAMES (ORS 648)

Registration (2 years)	$10 + $2 for each county registered
Renewal (2 years)	$10 + $2 for each county registered
Amendment	$10
Amendment to add counties	$10 + $2 for each added county
Cancellation	$10

Change of Registered Agent$10
Resignation of Registered Agent$10

MISCELLANEOUS FEES

Service of process	$20
Reservation of entity name	$10
Registration or Re-registration of Foriegn Corporate name	$100
*On-line computer printouts	$1
*Copies — document file (which includes articles and amendments to the articles) or assumed business name registrations	$5
*Copies — registered agent changes/resignations	$5
*Copies — renewal report for any entity	$5
*Certified copies of any of the above	$15
*Certificate (Existence, Authorization, Record)	$20
*Certificate of No Record	$5
*Statutes/Oregon Administrative Rules	$5

*These items must be paid in advance.

DOMESTIC ENTITIES

BUSINESS (ORS 60)		LIMITED PARTNERSHIPS (ORS 70)	
Filing	$50	Filing	$40
Annual	$30	Annual	$20
Reinstatement	$15	Reactivation	$30
Amendment/Restated/Merger	$10	Amendment	$10
Share Exchange/Revocation	$10	Restated Articles/Cancellation	$10
Correction/Amendment of Annual	$10		
Dissolution	$10		

FOREIGN ENTITIES

BUSINESS (ORS 60)		LIMITED PARTNERSHIPS (ORS 70)	
Authority	$440	Registration	$440
Annual	$220	Annual	$220
Reinstatement	$50	Reactivation	$50
Amendment/Merger	$10	Correction of Filing	$10
Correction	$10	Cancellation	$10
Amendment of Annual	$10		
Withdrawal	$10		

FORMS ARE AVAILABLE UPON REQUEST. PLEASE CALL (503) 378-2290

* Fees are subject to change without notice. Always check with the Corporations Division in Salem before filing (378-4166).

7

POST-INCORPORATION PROCEDURES

When you have received confirmation of incorporation from Salem, there are certain post-incorporation procedures that should be followed. These are purchasing a minute book, company seal, and share certificates, holding an organizational meeting of directors, issuing shares, opening a bank account for the company and getting the company's books into shape.

a. PURCHASE OF A MINUTE BOOK, COMPANY SEAL, AND SHARE CERTIFICATES

Keep minutes of all shareholders' and directors' meetings. File the minutes and other important corporate documents in the registered office or principal place of business.

Most corporations keep minutes and documents such as the Certificate of Incorporation, the articles and the bylaws as well as shareholder agreements in a minute book. A minute book is simply a binder that contains all of the above documents in a neat and orderly fashion. Its major use is as a record place for names and addresses of shareholders and the number of shares held. A minute book may be purchased from the office of the publisher. It is recommended that you get one, as then you will have all of the company documents together.

Oregon corporations do not require a seal, but banking practices may make one necessary. If you decide to have one, it need not state the corporate name. The seal can simply have the words "Oregon Incorporation" on it. You may select either the general type of seal or one with the corporate name on it.

b. MAKE YOUR BANKING ARRANGEMENTS

A corporation must have its own bank account and deposit, withdrawal, and checking arrangements because it is a separate legal entity. These arrangements should be made soon after incorporation by the directors. The bank you choose to deal with will provide you with the resolution forms necessary to open an account. Occasionally the bank will ask to see your articles or bylaws in order to ascertain the extent of corporate borrowing powers. Do not be surprised by this request.

c. HOLD A DIRECTORS' MEETING

The first meeting of directors is designed to launch the corporation into business. At the meeting you should —

(a) issue shares,

(b) elect officers,

(c) appoint a corporation banker,

(d) authorize transfer of assets into the corporation, and

(e) make any necessary tax elections (talk to IRS or your accountant).

Remember that it is the directors who sit in power and who theoretically (actually, in most close corporations) direct the corporation on all important issues. Whenever an important issue arises, it is resolved by the directors and is confirmed by the minutes of directors. Sample #12 shows the minutes of an actual meeting of directors. In most small close corporations these meetings are merely a formality and it is common to consent in writing to the standard items of procedure and file that consent in lieu of holding an actual meeting. Sample #13 is an illustration of a typical consent in lieu of an organizational meeting. It is in the package of forms available from the publisher. Notice of the first meeting must either be given (see Sample #14) or waived.

Subchapter S or section 1244 elections should be made at this meeting in order that they be effective. Section 1244 elections are illustrated in Samples #12, #13 and #14. Subchapter S election may be found in the minutes for a subchapter S election illustrated in Sample #3.

Remember to file the appropriate tax form with the tax authorities, as discussed in chapter 3. If these elections are made by companies that are unsuitable for this type of tax treatment, tax complications can occur. It is advisable, therefore, to obtain advice from an accountant experienced in corporate taxation before making either or both of these elections.

d. ADOPT THE BYLAWS

When you read the minutes of the organizational meeting of directors or the consent resolution in lieu of the organizational meeting, you will see a clause or resolution adopting bylaws. All Oregon corporations need bylaws to govern the internal workings of the corporation. These differ from the Articles of Incorporation in that the articles form the basic agreement of the incorporators.

The Business Corporation Act does not specify a certain form or terms to be included in bylaws, but your bylaws will be used by corporate officers and directors to determine the requirements for notices, meetings, duties of officers and other matters which may arise from time to time. Therefore, it is not necessarily a wasteful duplication to include in the bylaws some of the matters that are covered by statute or by the Articles of Incorporation.

In addition, because the bylaws can be changed more easily than the Articles of Incorporation, it is better to have all foreseeable contingencies covered in them. Sample #16 shows a set of bylaws that cover the important aspects of running a small business corporation. Omit any bylaws that are not applicable or add any that are necessary for your particular situation. All the items in Table #2 should be covered in your bylaws. The relevant sections of the law are given where applicable.

SAMPLE #12
MINUTES OF ORGANIZATIONAL MEETING

MINUTES OF ORGANIZATIONAL MEETING

OF BOARD OF DIRECTORS

OF

J & J PERSONNEL INC.

TIME AND PLACE: The organizational meeting of the Board of Directors named in the Articles of Incorporation of: J & J Personnel Inc. was held at 123 Incorporation Road, Portland, Oregon at 9:00 am, on the 10 th day of May, 199-, pursuant to a Waiver of Notice signed by each of the Directors.

PRESENT: John Doe presided over the meeting and appointed Jack Doe to act as Secretary of the meeting. Also present were:

The Waiver of Notice was presented to the meeting and was ordered filed with the minutes of the meeting.

ARTICLES OF INCORPORATION: The Chairman reported that the Corporation's Articles of Incorporation had been filed in the office of the Corporation Commissioner of the State of Oregon on the 15th day of April, 199-, and that a duplicate counterpart of the Articles of Incorporation, bearing the approval of the Secretary of State of Oregon and having attached the Certificate of Incorporation, was presented to the meeting, and the Secretary was instructed to place the copy of the articles and the Certificate of Incorporation in the minute book of the Corporation.

BYLAWS: A set of proposed Bylaws for the regulation and government of the affairs of the Corporation was presented to the meeting. After discussion, and upon motion duly made and seconded, the following resolution was unanimously adopted:

> RESOLVED: That the Bylaws in the form presented to this meeting are hereby approved and adopted as the Bylaws of the Corporation, and that the Secretary is directed to file them in the minute book.

ELECTION OF OFFICERS: The meeting was declared open for election of officers. After discussion, upon motion duly made and seconded, the following officers were unanimously elected to serve until the next annual meeting and until their respective successors are elected and qualified:

PRESIDENT: John Doe

SECRETARY-TREASURER Jack Doe

(Note: Only the President and Secretary are necessary. In a one-person company, the shareholder has both positions.)

SAMPLE #12 — Continued

*SECTION 1244 PLAN: The Board of Directors next considered the desirability of adopting a plan as a small business corporation under Section 1244 of the Internal Revenue Code, which under certain circumstances permits individual subscribing shareholders to take ordinary rather than capital losses if they sell their stock at a loss or if the Corporation is dissolved and they suffer a loss. After discussion, and upon motion duly made and seconded, the following resolution was unanimously adopted:

> RESOLVED: That the Plan of Stock Issuance in the form presented to this meeting is hereby approved and adopted by the Corporation, and that the Secretary is directed to file a copy of the Plan of Stock Issuance with the minutes of this meeting.

*Note: Optional. Before including this clause, see chapter 3 on Section 1244. If you use this form attach the terms of the Plan 1244 agreement to the minutes of your meeting.

SUBSCRIPTION OF STOCK OF COMPANY: After discussion, upon motion duly made and seconded the following resolution was unanimously adopted:

> RESOLVED: That the subscriptions of each of the following persons for the number of shares set forth opposite their name are accepted and upon payment to the Corporation of the amount set forth opposite a subscriber's name, a certificate for the number of shares set forth opposite his or her name shall be delivered to him or her.

NAME	SHARES	PURCHASE PRICE
John Doe	250 common shares	$250 (two hundred fifty)
Jack Doe	250 common shares	$250 (two hundred fifty)

PAID IN CAPITAL: The subscribers then each delivered their check in the amount specified above to the Corporation.

The Chairman announced that the Corporation had now received consideration of a value of at least $500 for the issuance of shares as required by the Articles of Incorporation and the Corporation is now authorized to transact business.

BANK ACCOUNT: It was considered advisable for the Corporation to establish a bank account with the Anywhere Branch of Savings Bank of Oregon. The bank's resolution form being presented to the meeting and, on motion duly made and seconded, the resolution incorporated therein was unanimously adopted. Two copies of the form were then executed and the Secretary was directed to deliver one copy to the bank and to file the other copy with the minutes of this meeting.

There being no further business to come before the meeting, the meeting was adjourned.

ATTEST:

Jack Doe
SECRETARY

John Doe
PRESIDENT

SAMPLE #13
CONSENT RESOLUTIONS IN LIEU OF ORGANIZATIONAL MEETING OF DIRECTORS

Consent to Action of Board of Directors in Lieu of Organizational Meeting of Directors of

J & J Personnel Inc.

We, the undersigned, being all of the initial Board of Directors named in the Articles of Incorporation, do hereby waive notice of the time and place of the organizational meeting and in its place consent to the following actions of the Board of Directors.

1. The undersigned consent to the filing of the Articles of Incorporation with the Certificate of Incorporation in the minute book of the corporation.

2. The bylaws attached hereto and incorporated by this reference are hereby adopted as the bylaws of this corporation.

3. The following are hereby elected as officers of the corporation to serve until their successors are elected and qualified.

President John Doe
*Vice-President
Secretary Jack Doe
Treasurer

4.* It is deemed desirable that the offer, sale and issuance of the corporation's stock be effectuated in such a manner that the qualified shareholders may receive the benefits of Section 1244 of the Internal Revenue Code and therefore the following plan to issue Section 1244 stock is hereby adopted by the Board of Directors:

(a) The plan as herein set forth shall be effective immediately.

(b) The corporation is authorized to offer and to issue 500 shares of common stock,

and all of such stock shall be issued subsequent to the date the plan becomes effective and for a period not to exceed two years from the date of adoption of the plan, or to the date when the corporation shall make a subsequent offering of any stock, whichever date shall occur first.

(c) During the period set forth in paragraph (b) above, the corporation shall offer and issue only such common stock.

(d) The maximum amount to be received by the corporation in consideration of the stock to be issued pursuant to this plan shall be $500,000.

(e) Such common stock shall be issued only for money or other property, provided such other property shall not be stock or securities.

(f) Such other action shall be taken by the corporation as shall qualify the stock offered and issued under this plan as "Section 1244 stock" as such term is defined in the Internal Revenue Code and the regulations issued thereunder, and the officers of the corporation are hereby authorized, empowered, and directed to do and perform any and all acts and deeds necessary to carry out such plan.

**Note: Only the President and Secretary are necessary, and a single person may hold multiple offices.*

**No.4 is optional, delete if not applicable to you.*

Self-Counsel Press Inc.
1704 N. State Street
Bellingham WA 98225
USA INC ORE (2-1) 88

SAMPLE #13 — Continued

5. The subscriptions of each of the following persons for the number of shares set forth opposite his or her name are accepted and upon payment to the corporation of the amount set forth opposite a subscriber's name, a certificate for the number of shares set forth opposite his or her name shall be delivered to the subscriber.

NAME	SHARES	PURCHASE PRICE
John Doe	150	$150 (one hundred fifty)
Jack Doe	150	$150 (one hundred fifty)

6. As the subscribers have delivered their checks for the specified amounts to the corporation, the undersigned agree that the corporation has now received consideration of a value of at least $300 for the issuance of shares.

7. The resolutions attached hereto and incorporated by this reference establishing the banks for the deposit of the corporation's funds are hereby unanimously adopted.

APPROVED and CONSENTED to as of May 10, 199-
(date)

John Doe [signature] John Doe

Jack Doe [signature] Jack Doe

(Directors sign here)

Self-Counsel Press Inc.
1704 N. State Street
Bellingham WA 98225
USA INC ORE (2-2) 88

SAMPLE #13 — Continued

RESOLUTION

"RESOLVED, that the President and the Secretary-Treasurer of the corporation, are hereby authorized to execute on behalf of the corporation any and all forms of bank resolutions dealing with corporate banking matters, including the establishing and maintaining of corporate bank accounts, which in their judgment from time to time may be required for the proper fiscal management of the corporation, including the designation thereon of such authorized signatures of corporate officers as may to them seem appropriate. The said officers may execute such banking resolution or resolutions as if authorized to do so by a specific resolution of the board of directors adopted on the date this resolution was adopted by the board.

DATED May 10, 199-

John Doe

Jack Doe

____

SAMPLE #14
FORMAL NOTICE OF ORGANIZATIONAL MEETING

NOTICE OF ORGANIZATIONAL MEETING
OF BOARD OF DIRECTORS

OF

J & J PERSONNEL INC.

John Doe

Jack Doe

The undersigned, being the incorporator of the corporation hereby gives the above named initial directors of the corporation notice of the organization meeting of the Board of Directors of the corporation to be held at 123 Incorporation Road on the 10th day of May, 199- .

EXECUTED and mailed this 26th day of April, 199- .

John Doe

Note: Instead of giving formal notice, you may prefer to add the following waiver of notice to the minutes of your meeting. "Notice of this meeting is hereby waived by the undersigned directors."

SAMPLE #15
PLAN OF SECTION 1244 STOCK ISSUANCE

PLAN OF STOCK ISSUANCE

OF

J & J PERSONNEL INC.

Plan of Stock Issuance, adopted by J & J Personnel Inc., an Oregon corporation:

A. The Corporation desires to issue pursuant to this plan not more than 1,000 shares of its common stock, which stock is intended to be "Section 1244" stock within the meaning of Section 1244 of the Internal Revenue Code of 1954.

B. The Corporation is as of the date hereof a "small business corporation" within the meaning of Section 1244 of the Internal Revenue Code of 1954.

C. The aggregate amount of money and other property to be received by the Corporation upon the issuance of the common stock pursuant to this plan plus the aggregate amount of money and other property heretofore received by the Corporation since the date of its incorporation, either for stock, as contributions to capital, or as paid-in surplus, does not exceed $500,000.

D. The aggregate amount of stock which may be offered under this plan plus the equity capital (as that phrase is defined in such Section 1244) of the Corporation at the date hereof does not exceed $1,000,000.

E. No portion of any prior offering of any stock of the Corporation is outstanding at the date hereof.

NOW, THEREFORE, the Corporation hereby adopts the following plan of stock issuance:

1. The Corporation hereby offers, pursuant to this plan 1,000 shares of its common stock at a subscription price to be established by the Board of Directors of the Corporation payable in cash or in property (not including stock or securities), for a total price of not in excess of $500,000 to a limited group of subscribers to be selected by the Board of Directors of the Corporation.

2. The period of this offer shall terminate on the 10th day of May, 199- unless sooner terminated by the Board of Directors. The offer may be accepted only by execution and delivering to the Corporation on or before said date a

written subscription to this plan and the payment in full of the purchase price on or before said date.

3. No other voluntary offers of any stock shall be made by the Corporation until all of the shares described herein have been issued or until the period of this offer shall have expired, or this plan shall have been expressly terminated by the Board of Directors, whichever event shall first occur.

4. The President and the Secretary of the Corporation are authorized and directed to issue and deliver to each new shareholder a stock certificate representing such stock as soon as practicable after receipt of such written subscription and the payment of such subscription price and in no event later than the close of business on the 10th day of May, 199-.

Jack Doe
DIRECTOR

John Doe
DIRECTOR

____
DIRECTOR

ATTEST:

John Doe
PRESIDENT

Jack Doe
SECRETARY-TREASURER

TABLE #2
BYLAW REQUIREMENTS

Items in the bylaws	Governing sections from the Oregon Business Corporation Act
(1) Annual meeting of shareholders	
Time and place	
Notice requirement	57.145
Fixing of the record date	57.150
Quorum	57.165
Order of business	
(2) Special shareholder meeting requirements	Same as above
(3) Voting rights and procedures	57.170, 57.175
Proxies	57.432 - 57.450
Cumulative voting	
(4) Shareholder action without meeting	
(5) Directors	
Qualifications	57.180, 57.200
Elections	57.231
Term of office	
Replacement	
Powers	
Compensation	
Indemnification	
Removal	57.211, 57.255
(6) Directors' meetings	
Regular and special	
Time and place	
Notice	
Quorum	
(7) Action by directors without meeting	
(8) Officers	
Designation	57.241
Qualification	57.236
Term of office	57.260
Removal	
Duties	
Compensation	
Indemnification	
(9) Committees of the board	57.206
Executive	
Finance	
Other	
(10) Execution of contracts	
(11) Corporate seal	
(12) Books and records	57.246
Directors and shareholder's right of inspection	
(13) Stock certificates	
Issuance	
Signatures	
Transfer	
(14) Closing of stock transfer books	
(15) Dividends and reserves	57.216, 57.221
(16) Fiscal year and audits	

SAMPLE #16
BYLAWS

Bylaws
of

J & J Personnel Inc.

ARTICLE 1 (Offices)

The principal office of the corporation shall be located at: 123 Incorporation Rd., Portland, OR.

The corporation may have such other offices, either within or without the State of Oregon, as the Board of Directors ("Board") may designate or as the business of the corporation may require from time to time.

ARTICLE 2 (Shareholders)

2.1. **Annual Meeting:** The annual meeting of the shareholders shall be held the first week of January in each year at the office of the corporation for the purpose of electing directors and transacting such other business as may come before the meeting. If the day fixed for the annual meeting is a legal holiday at the place of the meeting, the meeting shall be held on the next succeeding business day. If the election of directors is not held on the day designated for the annual meeting of the shareholders, or at any adjournment thereof, the election shall be held at a special meeting of the shareholders called as soon thereafter as practicable.

2.2. **Special Meetings:** The President or the Board may call special meetings of the shareholders for any purpose. At the request of the holders of not less than one-tenth of all of the outstanding shares of the corporation entitled to vote at the meeting, the President shall call a special meeting of the shareholders.

2.3. **Place of Meeting:** All meetings shall be held at the principal office of the corporation or at such other place within or without the State of Oregon designated by the Board or by a waiver of notice signed by all of the shareholders entitled to vote at the meeting.

2.4. **Notice of Meeting:** The President or Board when calling an annual or special meeting of shareholders shall cause to be delivered to each shareholder entitled to vote at the meeting either personally or by mail not less than 10 nor more than 50 days before the meeting written notice stating the place, day and hour of the meeting and, in the case of a special meeting, the purpose or purposes of which the meeting is called.

2.5. **Action by Shareholders Without a Meeting:** Any action required or permitted to be taken at a shareholders' meeting may be taken without a meeting if a written consent setting forth the action so taken is signed by all shareholders entitled to vote with respect to the subject matter thereof. Any such consent shall be inserted in the minute book as if it were the minutes of a shareholders' meeting.

2.6. **Quorum:** A majority of the outstanding shares of the corporation entitled to vote, represented in person or by proxy, shall constitute a quorum at a shareholders' meeting. If less than a majority of the outstanding shares are represented at a meeting, a majority of the shares so represented may adjourn the meeting from time to time without further notice. At an adjourned meeting at which a quorum is present or represented, any business may be transacted that might have been transacted at the meeting as originally notified. The shareholders present at a duly organized meeting may continue to transact business until adjournment, notwithstanding the withdrawal of enough shareholders to leave less than a quorum.

2.7. **Proxies:** At all shareholders' meetings a shareholder may vote by proxy executed in writing by the shareholder or by his attorney in fact. Such proxy shall be filed with the Secretary of the corporation before or at the time of the meeting. Unless otherwise provided in the proxy, a proxy shall be invalid after 11 months from the date of its execution.

2.8. **Voting of Shares:** Each outstanding share entitled to vote shall be entitled to one vote upon each matter submitted to a vote at a meeting of shareholders.

Optional. Delete if not applicable.

2.9. **Cumulative Voting:** Each shareholder entitled to vote at an election of directors may vote in person or by proxy the number of shares owned by him for as many persons as there are directors to be elected and for whose election he has a right to vote or he may cumulate his votes by distributing among one or more candidates as many votes as are equal to the number of such directors multiplied by the number of his shares.

1

Self-Counsel Press Inc.
1704 N. State Street
Bellingham WA 98225
USA INC ORE (3-1) 78

ARTICLE 3 (Board of Directors)

3.1. **General Powers:** The business and affairs of the corporation shall be managed by the Board.

Insert the number you choose.

3.2. **Number, Tenure and Qualifications:** The Board shall be composed of 2 directors, provided, however, that the number of directors may be changed from time to time to any number. If at any time the number of directors is less than three, the number of directors shall equal the number of shareholders. No decrease in the number of directors shall have the effect of shortening the term of any incumbent director. Each director shall hold office until the next annual meeting until his successor shall have been elected and qualifies unless he resigns or is removed. Directors need not be shareholders of the corporation.

3.3. **Regular Meetings:** A regular Board meeting shall be held without notice immediately after and at the same place as the annual meeting of shareholders. By resolution, the Board may provide the time and place either within or without the State of Oregon for holding additional regular meetings without other notice than such resolution.

3.4. **Special Meetings:** Special Board meetings may be called by or at the request of the President or any two directors. The person or persons authorized to call special meetings may fix any place either within or without the State of Oregon as the place for holding any special Board meeting called by them.

3.5. **Notice:** Written notice of each special Board meeting shall be delivered personally, telegraphed or mailed to each director at his business address at least two days before the meeting. If such notice is mailed, it shall be deemed to be delivered when deposited in the United States mail properly addressed, with postage prepaid. If the notice is telegraphed, it shall be deemed to be delivered when the content of the telegram is delivered to the telegraph office. The attendance of a director at a meeting shall constitute a waiver of notice of such meeting, except where a director attends a meeting for the express purpose of objecting to the transaction of any business because the meeting is not lawfully called or convened. Neither the business to be transacted at, nor the purpose of, any regular or special meeting of the Board need be specified in the notice or waiver of notice of such meeting.

3.6. **Quorum:** A majority of the directors shall constitute a quorum for the transaction of business at any Board meeting but, if less than such majority be present at a meeting, a majority of the directors present may adjourn the meeting from time to time without further notice.

3.7. **Manner of Acting:** The act of the majority of the directors present at a meeting at which a quorum is present shall be the act of the Board.

3.8. **Vacancies:** Any vacancy occurring on the Board may be filled by the affirmative vote of a majority of the remaining directors though less than a quorum of the Board. A director elected to fill a vacancy shall be elected for the unexpired term of his predecessor in office. Any directorship to be filled by reason of an increase in the number of directors shall be filled by election at an annual meeting or at a special shareholders' meeting called for that purpose.

3.9. **Removal:** At a meeting of shareholders called expressly for that purpose, one or more members of the Board (including the entire Board) may be removed, with or without cause, by a vote of the holders of a majority of the shares then entitled to vote on election of directors. (If less than the entire Board is to be removed, no one of the directors may be removed if the votes cast against his removal would be sufficient to elect him if then cumulatively voted at an election of the entire Board.)

3.10. **Compensation:** By Board resolution, directors may be paid their expenses, if any, of attendance at each Board meeting or a fixed sum for attendance at each Board meeting or a stated salary as director or any combination of the foregoing. No such payment shall preclude any director from serving the corporation in any other capacity and receiving compensation therefor.

3.11. **Presumption of Assent:** A director of the corporation present at a Board meeting at which action on any corporate matter is taken shall be presumed to have assented to the action taken unless his dissent is entered in the minutes of the meeting or unless he files his written dissent to such action with the person acting as the Secretary of the meeting before the adjournment thereof or unless he forwards such dissent by registered mail to the Secretary of the corporation immediately after the adjournment of the meeting. A director who voted in favor of such action may not dissent.

3.12. **Action by Directors without a Meeting:** Any action required or permitted to be taken at a meeting of the Board may be taken without a meeting if a written consent setting forth the action to be taken is signed by each of the directors. Any such written consent shall be inserted in the minute book as if it were the minutes of a Board meeting.

2

SAMPLE #16 — Continued

ARTICLE 4 (Officers)

Delete inapplicable positions. President and Secretary are necessary.

4.1. **Number:** The officers of the corporation shall be a President, one or more Vice-Presidents, a Secretary and a Treasurer, each of whom shall be elected by the Board. Such other officers and assistant officers as may be deemed necessary may be elected or appointed by the Board. Any two or more offices may be held by the same person, except the offices of President and Secretary provided that if there is only one shareholder/director, then he may be both President and Secretary.

4.2. **Election and Term of Office:** The officers of the corporation shall be elected annually by the Board at the Board meeting held after the annual meeting of the shareholders. If the election of officers is not held at such meeting, such election shall be held as soon thereafter as a Board meeting conveniently may be held. Each officer shall hold office until the next annual meeting and until his successor shall have been elected and qualified unless he resigns or is removed.

4.3. **Vacancies:** A vacancy in any office because of death, resignation, removal, disqualification or otherwise, may be filled by the Board for the unexpired portion of the term.

4.5. **President:** The President shall be the principal executive officer of the corporation and, subject to the Board's control, shall supervise and control all of the business and affairs of the corporation. When present, he shall preside over all shareholders' meetings and over all Board meetings. With the Secretary or other officer of the corporation authorized by the Board, he may sign certificates for shares of the corporation, deeds, mortgages, bonds, contract, or other instruments that the Board has authorized to be executed, except when the signing and execution thereof has been expressly delegated by the Board or by these Bylaws to some other officer or agent of the corporation or is required by law to be otherwise signed or executed by some other officer or in some other manner. In general, he shall perform all duties incident to the office of President and such other duties as may be prescribed by the Board from time to time.

4.6. **Vice-President:** In the absence of the President or in the event of his death, inability or refusal to act, the Vice-President (or in the event of more than one Vice-President, the Vice-President who was first elected to such office) shall perform the duties of the President, and when so acting, shall have all the powers of and be subject to all the restrictions upon the President. Vice-Presidents shall perform such other duties as from time to time may be assigned to them by the President or by the Board.

Note: Seal is not mandatory in Oregon

4.7. **Secretary:** The Secretary shall: (a) keep the minutes of shareholders' and Board meetings in one or more books provided for that purpose; (b) see that all notices are duly given in accordance with the provisions of these Bylaws or as required by law; (c) be custodian of the corporate records and of the seal of the corporation and see that the seal of the corporation is affixed to all documents, the execution of which on behalf of the corporation under its seal is duly authorized; (d) keep a register of the post office address of each shareholder as furnished to the Secretary by each shareholder; (e) sign with the President, or Vice-President certificates for shares of the corporation, the issuance of which has been authorized by resolution of the Board; (f) have general charge of the stock transfer books of the corporation; and (g) in general perform all duties incident to the office of Secretary and such other duties as from time to time may be assigned to him by the President or by the Board.

4.8. **Treasurer:** If required by the Board, the Treasurer shall give a bond for the faithful discharge of his duties in such sum and with such surety or sureties as the Board shall determine. He shall have charge and custody of and be responsible for all funds and securities of the corporation; receive and give receipts for moneys due and payable to the corporation from any source whatsoever, and deposit all such moneys in the name of the corporation in such banks, trust companies or other depositaries as shall be selected in accordance with the provisions of these Bylaws and in general perform all of the duties incident to the office of Treasurer and such other duties as from time to time may be assigned to him by the President or by the Board.

4.9. **Salaries:** The salaries of the officers shall be fixed from time to time by the Board, and no officer shall be prevented from receiving such salary by reason of the fact that he is also a director of the corporation.

ARTICLE 5 (Contracts, Loans, Checks and Deposits)

5.1. **Contracts:** The Board may authorize any officer or officers, agent or agents, to enter into any contract or execute and deliver any instrument in the name of and on behalf of the corporation, and such authority may be general or confined to specific instances.

5.2. **Loans:** No loans shall be contracted on behalf of the corporation and no evidences of indebtedness shall be issued in its name unless authorized by a resolution of the Board. Such authority may be general or confined to specific instances.

3

5.3. **Loans to Officers and Directors:** No loans shall be made by the corporation to its officers or directors, unless first approved by the holders of three-fourths of the shares, and no loans shall be made by the corporation secured by its shares.

5.4. **Checks, drafts, etc.:** All checks, drafts or other orders for the payment of money, notes or other evidences of indebtedness issued in the name of the corporation, shall be signed by such officer or officers, agent or agents, of the corporation and in such manner as from time to time determined by resolution of the Board.

5.5. **Deposits:** All funds of the corporation not otherwise employed shall be deposited from time to time to the credit of the corporation in such banks, trust companies or other depositaries as the Board may select.

ARTICLE 6 (Certificates for Shares and Their Transfer)

6.1. **Certificates for Shares:** Certificates representing shares of the corporation shall be signed by the President or Vice-President and by the Secretary and shall include on their face written notice:

> "The shares represented by this certificate are subject to all the terms and conditions of the Bylaws and Articles of Incorporation of J & J Personnel Inc. , and any amendments thereof, copies of which are on file at the office of the corporation."

All certificates shall be consecutively numbered or otherwise identified. The name and address of the person to whom the shares represented thereby are issued, with the number of shares and date of issue, shall be entered on the stock transfer books of the corporation. All certificates surrendered to the corporation for transfer shall be canceled and no new certificate shall be issued until the former certificate for a like number of shares shall have been surrendered and canceled, except that in case of a lost, destroyed or mutilated certificate, a new one may be issued therefor upon such terms and indemnity to the corporation as the Board may prescribe.

6.2. **Transfer of Shares:** Transfer of shares of the corporation shall be made only on the stock transfer books of the corporation by the holder of record thereof or his legal representative, who shall furnish proper evidence of authority to transfer, or by his attorney in fact authorized by power of attorney duly executed and filed with the Secretary of the corporation, and on surrender for cancellation of the certificates for such shares. The person in whose name shares stand on the books of the corporation shall be deemed by the corporation to be the owner thereof for all purposes.

6.3. **Share Transfer Restriction.** No shareholder shall sell or otherwise dispose of any of the shares in the corporation, now or hereafter acquired by him, except under the following terms and conditions:

(a) A person (herein called the "proposing transferor") desiring to transfer any share or shares in the corporation shall give notice in writing (herein called "transfer notice") to the corporation that he desires to transfer the same. The transfer notice shall specify the price, which shall be expressed in lawful money of the United States and the terms of payment upon which the proposing transferor is prepared to transfer the share or shares and shall constitute the corporation his agent for the sale thereof to any shareholder or shareholders of the corporation at the price and upon the terms of payment so specified. The transfer notice shall also state whether or not the proposing transferor has had an offer to purchase the shares or any of them from, or proposes to sell the shares or any of them to, any particular person or persons who are not shareholders, and if so the names and addresses of such persons shall be specified in the transfer notice. The transfer notice shall constitute an offer by the proposing transferor to the other shareholder of the corporation holding shares of the class or classes included in the transfer notice and shall not be revocable except with the sanction of the directors. If the transfer notice pertains to shares of more than one class then the consideration and terms of payment for each class of shares shall be stated separately in the transfer notice.

(b) The directors shall forthwith upon receipt thereof transmit the transfer notice to each of the shareholders, other than the proposing transferor, holding shares of the class or classes set forth in the transfer notice and request the shareholder to whom the transfer notice is sent to state in writing within 14 days from the date of the transfer notice whether he is willing to accept any, and if so, the maximum number of shares he is willing to accept at the price and upon the terms specified in the transfer notice. A shareholder shall only be entitled to purchase shares of the class or classes held by him.

(c) Upon the expiration of the 14-day notice period referred to in article 6.3 (b), if the directors shall have received from the shareholders entitled to receive the transfer notice sufficient acceptances to take up the full number of shares offered by the transfer notice and, if the transfer notice includes shares of more than one class, sufficient acceptances from the members of each class to take up the full number of shares of each class offered by the transfer notice, the directors shall thereupon apportion shares so offered among the shareholders so accepting and so far as may be, pro rata, according

4

to the number of shares held by each of them respectively, and in the case of more than one class of shares, then pro rata in respect of each class. If the directors shall not have received sufficient acceptances as aforesaid, they may, but only with the consent of the proposing transferor who shall not be obliged to sell to shareholders in the aggregate less than the total number of shares of one or more classes of shares offered by the transfer notice, apportion the shares so offered among the shareholders so accepting so far as may be according to the number of shares held by each respectively but only up to the amount accepted by such shareholders respectively. Upon any such apportionment being made, the proposing transferor shall be bound upon payment of the price to transfer the shares to the respective shareholders to whom the directors have apportioned same. If, in any case, the proposing transferor, having become so bound fails in transferring any share, the corporation may receive the purchase money for that share and shall upon receipt cause the name of the purchasing shareholders to be entered in the register as the holder of the shares and cancel the certificate of the share held by the proposed transferor, whether the same shall be produced to the corporation or not, and shall hold such purchase money in trust for the proposing transferor. The receipt of the corporation for the purchase money shall be a good discharge to the purchasing shareholders and after his name has been entered in the register the validity of the proceedings shall not be questioned by any person.

(d) In the event that some or all of the shares offered shall not be sold under the preceding articles within the 14-day period referred to in article 6.3 (b), the proposing transferor shall be at liberty for a period of 90 days after the expiration of that period to transfer such of the shares so offered as are not sold to any person provided that he shall not sell them at a price less than that specified in the transfer notice or on terms more favorable to a purchaser than those specified in the transfer notice.

(e) The provisions as to transfer contained in this article shall not apply:

(i) if before the proposed transfer of shares is made, the transferor shall obtain consents to the proposed transfer from members of the corporation, who at the time of the transfer are the registered holders of two-thirds or more of the issued shares of the class to be transferred to the corporation or if the shares comprise more than one class, then from the registered holders of two-thirds or more of the shares of each class to be transferred and such consent shall be taken to be a waiver of the application of the preceding articles as regards such transfer; or

(ii) to a transfer of shares desired to be made merely for the purpose of effectuating the appointment of a new trustee for the owner thereof, provided that it is proved to the satisfaction of the Board that such is the case.

(f) Nothing herein shall preclude any shareholder from transferring by gift or devise any shares to spouse or any child or children of the shareholder.

ARTICLE 7 (Fiscal Year)

The fiscal year of the corporation shall be the calendar year.

ARTICLE 8 (Seal)

The Seal of this corporation shall consist of the name of the corporation, the state of its incorporation and the year of its incorporation.

ARTICLE 9 (Waiver of Notice)

Whenever any notice is required to be given to any shareholder or director of the corporation under the provisions of these Bylaws or under the provisions of the Articles of Incorporation or under the provisions of the Oregon Business Corporation Act, a waiver thereof in writing, signed by the person or persons entitled to such notice, whether before or after the time stated therein, shall be deemed equivalent to the giving of such notice.

ARTICLE 10 (Indemnification)

To the full extent permitted by the Oregon Business Corporation Act the corporation shall indemnify any person who was or is a party or is threatened to be made a party to any civil, criminal, administrative or investigative action, suit or proceeding (whether brought by or in the right of the corporation or otherwise) by reason of the fact that he is or was a director or officer of the corporation, or is or was serving at the request of the corporation as a director or officer of another corporation, against expenses (including attorneys' fees), judgments, fines and liabilities, reasonably incurred by or imposed upon him in connection with or resulting from any claim, action, suit, or proceeding, provided that he acted in good faith and in a manner he reasonably believed to be in or not opposed to the best interests of the corporation. The termination of any action, suit, or proceeding by judgment, order, settlement, or conviction or upon a

5

plea of *nolo contendere* or its equivalent shall not, of itself, create a presumption that the person did not act in good faith and in a manner which he reasonably believed to be in, or not opposed to, the best interests of the corporation. The board of directors may obtain insurance on behalf of any person who is or was a director, officer, employee, or agent against any liability arising out of his status as such, whether or not the corporation would have power to indemnify him against such liability. The Board of Directors may, at any time, approve indemnification under the Oregon Business Corporation Act, of any other person which the corporation has the power to indemnify. The indemnification provided by this section shall not be deemed exclusive of any other rights to which a person may be entitled as a matter of law or by contract.

ARTICLE 11 (Amendments)

These Bylaws may be altered, amended or repealed and new Bylaws may be adopted by the Board at any regular or special meeting of the Board.

ADOPTED BY THE BOARD OF DIRECTORS this 10th day of May , 199- .

John Doe
DIRECTOR

Jack Doe
DIRECTOR

DIRECTOR

e. ISSUE SHARE CERTIFICATES

1. General points

The issuing and canceling of shares is a relatively simple affair because the form of share certificate is already prepared for you. You should be careful, however, to distinguish between the initial issue of shares on incorporation, subsequent issues out of the treasury (i.e., from the unissued "pool"), and simple transfers of already issued shares from one person to another. All three of these dealings involve different operations. Fortunately, the simplest operation comes first.

You should note the following general points regarding shares.

(a) For the average small corporation, a relatively few share certificates will suffice for normal purposes. This is because there are usually only a few shareholders and each share certificate can represent the total number of shares held by each person (because you do not need a separate certificate for each share).

(b) Share certificates should, whenever possible, remain in the minute book because if they are sent to the individual shareholder, some will inevitably be lost and you will then be faced with the annoying problem of replacing lost share certificates.

(c) Share certificates no longer have to be issued under the seal of the company, but they must be signed by at least one director or officer. Any other signatures may be printed or mechanically reproduced.

(d) Share certificates should be numbered consecutively in the space provided at the top of the certificate.

(e) The remaining information needed can be ascertained by closely examining article 6.1 of the bylaws and the sample certificate (see Sample #21).

(f) To cancel shares, simply write the word "canceled" across the face of the certificate and staple it shut on top of the tab or stub of the certificate.

(g) Last, but certainly not least, you must be sure to prepare the appropriate directors' minutes confirming the issuance, transfer, or cancellation of shares. Actually, there should never be a cancellation unless there is, at the same time, a transfer so the two would be incorporated in the same minutes.

An example of the resolution needed to issue shares out of the treasury can be found in the minutes of the organizational meeting of the board of directors (Sample #12).

2. Subsequent issue or allotment of shares

Suppose the directors decide to issue additional shares not previously issued from the corporate treasury. The existing shareholders have first chance at them.

Oregon law allows existing shareholders pre-emptive rights on new issues of shares unless the Articles of Incorporation state differently.

To make sure that existing shareholders can exercise their pre-emptive rights, each shareholder must sign a waiver (see Sample #17), or must at least receive a Notice of Offer to Allot Shares (see Sample #18). (Allotting shares is another way of saying issuing shares out of the treasury.) Any shareholder who does not want to purchase new shares should sign the waiver in order to show refusal.

SAMPLE #17
WAIVER OF RIGHTS

Shareholder of J & J Personnel Inc. *(company name)* has waived and hereby waives the right of the undersigned to receive an offer with respect to the allotment of 500 *(total number of shares issued)* common shares in the capital of the corporation at a price of $1 per share to Woody B. Stockholder which is proposed by the directors of the company.

John Doe

SAMPLE #18
NOTICE OF OFFER TO ALLOT SHARES

TO: Shareholders of

J & J Personnel Inc.

TAKE NOTICE that the directors of J & J Personnel Inc. propose to allot to Woody B. Stockholder of 321 Investor's Avenue, Portland, Oregon *(address)* a total of 1,000 common shares in the capital of the corporation, or the balance thereof not taken up by the shareholders of the corporation pursuant to the following offer, for subscription price of $1 per share, payable in cash on or before allotment.

The directors hereby offer 250 common shares to the holders of common shares in the capital of the corporation pro rata to their respective holdings of common shares in the company as of the date hereof to the closest number of whole shares, excluding fractions, at a price of $1 per share, payable in cash on or before allotment. This offer may be accepted by mailing by prepaid registered post or by delivering to the company at 123 Incorporation Road, Portland, Oregon, the attached form of acceptance within 14 days of the date of this notice, following which period this offer expires.

If the shareholders will not sign waivers, then all shareholders should be given Notices of Offer to Allot Shares.

All shareholders who want to purchase new shares will sign and file the form in Sample #19.

Finally the minutes of the meeting of directors confirming the issues should be drawn up.

In Oregon, the law also allows the corporation to create and issue options to purchase stock. If the options are not given to existing shareholders generally, then the options must be approved by an affirmative vote of the majority of the shareholders of record.

Your local courthouse or business library should have precedents or guides for you to follow in drawing up an option. Otherwise, your accountant can help. At any rate, notifying shareholders of options to purchase should not be too different from notifying them of allotments. Most small businesses will not become concerned with options until they become well established and prosperous or unusual circumstances arise.

SAMPLE #19
SHAREHOLDERS' ACCEPTANCE

The undersigned holder of common shares in J & J Personnel Inc. hereby accepts the offer of allotment of common shares set out in the notice at a price and on terms therein set forth to the extent of 250 common shares of the pro rata portion of the undersigned in accordance with the terms of said offer, whichever is the lesser.

DATED: December 20, 199- .

Jack Doe

(Signature of Shareholder)

3. Transfers of shares between shareholders

Ordinarily, the Articles of Incorporation or the bylaws will set out the method for transferring shares. In general, this means that the selling shareholder should notify the secretary or treasurer of the corporation of the transfer of shares and instruct him or her to make note of the transfers in the corporate books and records.

In the case of a corporation that uses the illustrated bylaws (see Sample #16), the sale of shares by a shareholder is specifically restricted. Other agreements between shareholders may also place restrictions on sale and/or transfer of shares. Such restrictions give shareholders the right of first refusal to purchase the seller's shares and also give the remaining shareholders the right to purchase them on a pro rata basis as regards other shareholders. If all or some of the shareholders decline to accept the offer, the person offering the shares may —

(a) decline to sell the shares not accepted,

(b) offer the remaining shares to shareholders who accepted the offer in the first instance,

(c) sell the remaining shares to third parties.

If your articles, bylaws, or agreement with other shareholders require the giving to the remaining shareholders a first right of refusal, Sample #20 is a suggested form to use in giving notice of sale. Sample #22 shows a share certificate transfer.

SAMPLE #20
NOTICE OF OFFER TO TRANSFER SHARES

NOTICE TO:

John Doe and Woody B. Stockholder *(other shareholders)* and:

TO:

J & J Personnel Inc. *(corporation)*

TAKE NOTICE that Jack Doe desires to sell 500 common shares of the corporation for the price of $2 per share payable in cash on transfer date.

AND FURTHER TAKE NOTICE that this notice hereby empowers J & J Personnel Inc. to be my agent in transfer of said shares to any member or members of the corporation. *(See Article 6.3(a) of bylaws.)*

AND FURTHER TAKE NOTICE that this notice hereby empowers J & J Personnel Inc. *(name of corporation)* in transferring said shares.

DATED: December 20, 199- .

Jack Doe

(Signature of Transferor)

SAMPLE #21
SHARE CERTIFICATE

NUMBER

SHARES

the State of Oregon

J & J Personnel Inc.

Capital Stock Total 500

This Certifies that John Doe is the owner of 150 Shares of the Capital Stock of J & J Personnel Inc. transferable only on the books of the Corporation by the holder hereof in person or by Attorney upon surrender of this Certificate properly endorsed.

IN WITNESS WHEREOF, the said Corporation has caused this Certificate to be signed by its duly authorized officers and its Corporate Seal to be hereunto affixed this 10th day of May A.D. 199-

CERTIFICATE

No.

For 150 Shares

Issued to John Doe

Dated May 10 199-

FROM WHOM TRANSFERRED

Dated 19

No. Original Certificate	No. Original Shares	No. of Shares Transferred

Received Certificate No.

For Shares

this day of 19

SAMPLE #21
(Back)

The shares represented by this certificate are subject to all terms and conditions of the Bylaws and Articles of Incorporation of J & J Personnel Inc and any amendments thereto, copies of which are on file at the office of the Corporation.

Certificate for 150 Shares Capital Stock

Issued to John Doe

Dated May 10, 199-

For Value Received, ______ *hereby sell, assign and transfer unto* ______

______ *Shares of the Capital Stock represented by the within Certificate, and do hereby irrevocably constitute and appoint* ______

to transfer the said Stock on the books of the within named Corporation with full power of substitution in the premises.

Dated ______ *19* ___

In presence of

______ ______

NOTICE. THE SIGNATURE OF THIS ASSIGNMENT MUST CORRESPOND WITH THE NAME AS WRITTEN UPON THE FACE OF THE CERTIFICATE, IN EVERY PARTICULAR, WITHOUT ALTERATION OR ENLARGEMENT, OR ANY CHANGE WHATEVER.

SAMPLE #22
SHARE CERTIFICATE TRANSFER

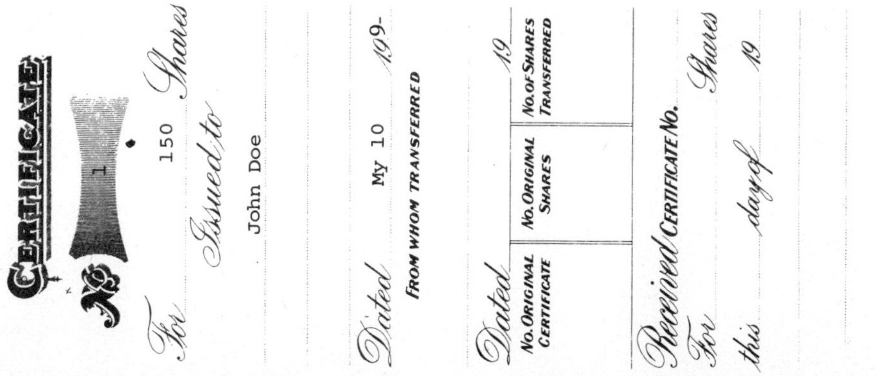

SAMPLE #22
(Back)

The shares represented by this certificate are subject to all terms and conditions of the Bylaws and Articles of Incorporation of J & J Personnel Inc., and any amendments thereto, copies of which are on file at the office of the Corporation.

Certificate for 150 Shares Capital Stock

Issued to John Doe

Dated May 10, 199-

For Value Received, I *hereby sell, assign and transfer unto* Jack Doe

all 150 (one hundred fifty) *Shares of the Capital Stock represented by the within Certificate, and do hereby irrevocably constitute and appoint* Joe Doe *to transfer the said Stock on the books of the within named Corporation with full power of substitution in the premises.*

Dated December 20 *19*9-

In presence of

Walter Witness   John Doe

NOTICE: THE SIGNATURE OF THIS ASSIGNMENT MUST CORRESPOND WITH THE NAME AS WRITTEN UPON THE FACE OF THE CERTIFICATE, IN EVERY PARTICULAR, WITHOUT ALTERATION OR ENLARGEMENT OR ANY CHANGE WHATEVER.

4. Who takes title to shares?

The name in which you take title to the corporate shares depends on your particular circumstances.

(a) If you are unmarried and will own 100% of the shares, take title to the shares in your name alone. This is your "separate property."

(b) If you are married you may also take title in your and your spouse's names as tenants by the entirety. This means that upon the death of one spouse, the surviving spouse will automatically become the sole owner and take title to the shares. In this case, the shares are not subject to probate.

f. TRANSFERRING ASSETS TO THE NEW CORPORATION

1. The lease

In many instances, an incorporator of a new corporation wants to sell furniture, fixtures, equipment, supplies, and sometimes real estate to the corporation. Unless the property sold to the corporation is actually paid for in cash, the incorporator may run the risk of not being paid in full for the property in the event the corporation should encounter financial difficulties, go out of business, or become bankrupt. In such a case, the seller would take an actual loss.

An alternative to selling personal or real property to the corporation is for the incorporator to lease such property to the corporation on a long-term basis at fair and reasonable rates. The amount of rent paid by the corporation is a business expense and is tax deductible by the corporation.

All leases with the corporation must be authorized by a resolution of the board of directors and be recorded in the minutes of the corporation. It is important that such leases provide that in the event of the bankruptcy of the corporation or its ceasing to do business, the leased property shall be returned to the lessors. The purpose of this type of an arrangement is to protect the lessor and prevent creditors of the corporation from reaching the leased property.

Remember, it is very easy to put assets into a corporation but sometimes difficult to get them out.

2. Organizations falling under section 351 of the Internal Revenue Code

When a corporation is formed, neither the transferor (you) of the property nor the recipient (your corporation) may recognize or claim a loss or gain if —

(a) the property is transferred to the corporation in exchange for shares only, and

(b) if you, the transferor, have control of the corporation immediately after the transfer takes place.

Section 351 of the Internal Revenue Code allows you to transfer whatever assets you want to your own corporation free of federal tax so long as you meet the criteria listed above.

To properly fall within the section, you must assign all rights in the property to the corporation. This means that the corporation usually has the right to sell or otherwise dispose of the goods. Special tax problems can arise when trademarks, franchises, and trade names are transferred to a company, and they should be given careful attention.

In order to have "control" within the scope of section 351, you must own at least 80% of the total combined voting power of all classes of stock entitled to vote and at least 80% of the total number of shares of all other classes of stock. Therefore, immediately after you have transferred assets to the corporation in exchange for shares alone you must own 80% or more of the total combined voting power of all classes of stock carrying voting rights.

You should be aware that problems can arise when the corporation assumes your liabilities along with your assets. The assumption of liabilities by the corporation merely reduces the adjusted basis of the stock received by you in the exchange (i.e., the stock is valued less). Where the nature of the liability and other circumstances indicate that you made the transfer in order to avoid tax or for some reason that was not a bona fide business purpose, then the transaction will be viewed as one that gives rise to tax liability.

Where the liabilities encumbering the property or assumed by the corporation exceed the total (aggregate) adjusted basis of all the property transferred, the excess is to be considered as a gain enjoyed by the transferor. This can be an expensive trap for unwary self-incorporators.

I might also mention that the transfer of stock in exchange for your services to the corporation and the transfer of assets in return for corporate notes (promissory notes) has to be handled with care in order to fall within the exemptions provided by section 351. These last types of transfer, however, should not be too common in the typical one-person or close corporation.

Basically, when you sell your asset to your corporation, the corporation must give something back in return as a payment for the debt. Some people prefer to receive a debt obligation rather than shares in exchange for their asset because when the corporation pays off its debts the money is considered as the repayment of a loan. If you receive shares your assets are forever tied up in the corporation, and you will receive no direct benefits unless the corporation is wound up and the assets are sold at a profit, which is highly unlikely. A common form of payment is the demand note, as shown in Sample #23.

A note like this can be prepared on behalf of the corporation in favor of each person transferring assets into the corporation.

As you can see, John Doe is entitled to "demand" payment at any time. What is to stop Mr. Doe from demanding payment immediately? First, he is not likely to demand payment unless he knows there are sufficient funds in the corporation's bank account to pay him. Second, if he had to sue it would be tantamount to suing himself since he is the part owner of the "entity." Consequently, a demand note payable to a shareholder-director of an incorporated partnership is usually a relatively safe proposition.

Usually an informal agreement between the working "partners" as to where and when the notes should be presented for payment is quite sufficient.

If the corporation pays interest on the note to Mr. Doe, he has to pay tax on it. Interest payments made to the holder of the note are taxable in his hands. The principal amount is not taxable as it is analagous to the repayment of a loan made to the company.

There is one major taxable risk in transferring assets to a company. If the corporation goes bankrupt or has judgments registered against it, the assets may be subject to seizure by creditors, in which case the debt owed to you by the corporation would be relegated to general creditor status, and you would have to share in the proceeds of the resale of the assets along with the other creditors.

The following is an example of the type of resolution you should file in your corporate records if you elect to transfer

SAMPLE #23
DEMAND NOTE

$2,000 April 30, 199-

ON DEMAND after the above date the corporation promises to pay to the order of John Doe at Anywhere, Oregon, Two Thousand Dollars ($2,000) with interest at the rate of ten percent (10%) per annum, as well after as before maturity, FOR VALUE RECEIVED.

J & J PERSONNEL INC.

Per: John Doe
President

Jack Doe.
Secretary

assets to your corporation via promissory note.

> IT WAS RESOLVED that the corporation purchase a motor vehicle and other equipment from the shareholder-director John Doe namely: 1983 Chevrolet, Serial Number 1234567B89 and that the said purchases be secured by promissory notes.
>
> IT WAS RESOLVED that the corporation execute the said promissory note in such manner as required to give full effect to the transaction hereinbefore decribed.

Of course, you would alter it if you were receiving shares instead of a promissory note. Afterwards, you would contact the Motor Vehicles Division in order to change the registration of the motor vehicle involved in the transfer.

Whatever method of transferring assets you use, be sure all transactions are accurately and fully documented. When transferring assets, it is certainly worthwhile to consult a tax accountant to avoid tax problems.

g. BUSINESS LICENSES

Many businesses and trades must meet qualifications established by the state, county, and city where the business is located. All of these requirements would have to be met by you even if you had hired an attorney to process your incorporation for you. As the purpose of issuing city and county licenses is mainly to raise revenue, practically all businesses are required to obtain a city or county license.

For information regarding a city license, telephone either the city clerk or the city licensing department. Information regarding county licenses is available from the county licensing department or the county tax collector, licensing division. The exact names for these agencies may vary throughout the state. However, an inquiry at the city hall or county administration office respectively, will direct you to the proper agency. For more information on licenses and other permits needed to start a business, please refer to *Starting a Successful Business on the West Coast,* another title in the Self-Counsel series.

In Portland the application for a business license is filed with the Business Licenses Division (see Sample #24).

h. REGISTRATION

New employers in Oregon must register with the state. The Combined Employer's Registration Report form includes information required of new employers for the Oregon Department of Revenue, the Employment Division and the Workers' Compensation Department. The same form can also be used to register for the Tri-Met and Lane County transit district taxes (see Sample #25).

This registration must be completed before the first paychecks are issued. An employer account number is assigned to each employer.

The state of Oregon publishes a very helpful booklet, *Information for Oregon Employers,* which contains the form and information about withholding tax, employment tax, transit district taxes, Multnomah County business tax, and workers' compensation insurance. You should get a copy of it before you begin business.

i. WITHHOLDING LAW IN OREGON

Every employer in Oregon must withhold tax from wages paid to an employee. The withheld tax is collected by the Oregon Department of Revenue, which regularly mails forms to registered employers. For detailed information about the withholding and reporting requirements, contact your nearest Department of Revenue field office. Do this as soon as possible as there are reporting requirements that must be met. Also, the office can tell you if your employees will be exempt.

SAMPLE #24
PORTLAND BUSINESS LICENSE FORM

BUSINESS LICENSES DIVISION
203 CITY HALL
1220 S.W. 5TH AVENUE
PORTLAND, OREGON 97204
248-4066

APPLICATION FOR CITY BUSINESS LICENSE

PLEASE PRINT OR TYPE **PLEASE PRINT OR TYPE**

1. To be issued to P & P Printing Inc.
(Name of owner, partners or corporation) (First name, middle name and last name of individuals)

2. Check one: ☐ Individual Proprietorship ☐ Partnership ☒ Corporation
☐ Professional Corporation ☐ Sub-Chapter "S" Corporation ☐ Other ______

3. List owner, partners or corporate officers

	Title	Residence address	Phone number
Jack Printer	president	1000 B Street, Yourtown, OR	999-1111
Jane Printer	secretary	1000 C Street, Yourtown, OR	111-9999

4. Assumed business name used (if any) N/A

5. Business Address 1000 A Street (Number and street) Portland, Oregon 97000 (City, State and Zip) 990-0000 (Business phone number)

List additional business locations on reverse side.

6. Name and address of property owner of above location/s ______

7. Mailing address if different than Line 5 ______

8. Business Description printing
(Indicate type of goods sold & designate whether retail, wholesale, etc. or service performed)

9. First date of doing business in City of Portland March 15, 199-

10. Are books to be kept on a calendar ____ or fiscal X year? If fiscal, state ending date March 31

11. Is this a new business venture? yes or a previously licensed business purchased by you? ____

12. If previously licensed business, from whom purchased? ______

13. Have you ever been licensed in Portland before? No What year? ____ Address ______

14. Current number of employees (include yourself) working in the City of Portland 4 (four)

Reasonable estimated license fee (to accompany application) is calculated at the rate of 2.3% of net income subject to fee.

MINIMUM FEE IS $25.00 and is subject to adjustment upon renewal.

The application with a check payable to CITY TREASURER must be mailed to: **License Division, Room 203, City Hall, Portland, OR 97204.**

The term "license" as used in the ordinance is not to be construed to mean a permit. The Business License Fee is for revenue purposes, and is not a regulatory permit fee. The payment of a license fee and the acceptance of such fee and issuance of a license by the city does not entitle a licensee to carry on any business not in compliance with all applicable requirements of state, federal, municipal or other law.

The undersigned declares under penalty of making a false certificate that the information given in this report is true.

DATE March 16, 199- SIGNATURE Jack Printer
(Owner, Partner, Corporate Officer or other duly authorized representative)

L12 REV. 2/77

SAMPLE #25
COMBINED EMPLOYERS' REGISTRATION REPORT

Mail completed form to:
Oregon Department of Revenue
Box 14800
Salem, OR 97309

COMBINED
EMPLOYER'S REGISTRATION REPORT
Oregon Withholding Tax
Oregon Employment Tax
Transportation District Taxes

1. Business Name P & P Printing Inc. Phone No. 990-0000

2. Principal location of business
1000 A Street
Portland, Oregon 97000

3. Mailing address if different from Item 2.

4. Accountant or Bookkeeping Service
Larry Ledger & Co.
1000 D. Street
Anytown, Oregon 97001

Your Federal I.D. Number 000000

Do you wish to have your reporting forms mailed directly to your accountant? ☐ Yes ☒ No

5. WITHHOLDING TAX Filing Status (Check one)
☒ Monthly (withholding tax will exceed $500.00 per quarter)
☐ Quarterly (withholding tax will be less than $500.00 per quarter)
☐ Semi-Annual (withholding tax will be less than $150.00 per quarter)

Date employes will be FIRST PAID: March 31, 199-
Date first Oregon employe hired: Month 3 Day 15 Year 199-

6. EMPLOYMENT TAX
a. In what calendar quarter did/will your payroll first exceed $225.00? Quarter first Year 199-
b. Will you have at least one employe (full or part time) in each of 18 weeks during the calendar year? ☒ Yes ☐ No

7. TRANSPORTATION DISTRICT TAXES
(For employers who will have employes working in the Transit Districts)
☒ Tri-Met (Multnomah, Clackamas, and Washington counties)
☐ Lane Transit District (Lane County)

Date employes first paid for services within the district
Tri-Met March 31, 199-
LTD

8. WORKERS' COMPENSATION INSURANCE
Insurance Company handling your Workers' Compensation insurance Risky Insurance Co.

9. Describe the nature of your business Printing

10. Type of ownership ☐ Individual ☐ Partnership ☒ Corporation
If Corporation – Domestic ☒ Foreign ☐ If foreign, State in which incorporated

11. Did you acquire an established business? ☐ Yes ☒ No Date of acquisition
Did you acquire the entire employing enterprise of the previous owner? ☐ Yes ☐ No

FORMER BUSINESS: Name Revenue Acct. No.
Address Employment Acct. No.
Owner

12. IDENTIFICATION OF OWNERS, PARTNERS, CORPORATION OFFICERS, ETC.

Social Security Number	Name (given name in full)	Residence Address & Phone No.	Title	% Ownership
000-00-0000	Jack Albert Printer	1000 B Street, Yourtown, OR 999-111	Pres.	50
111-11-1111	Jane Ann Printer	1000 C Street, Yourtown, OR 111-9999	Secy.	50

150-211-055 (Rev. 12/77) (over)

SAMPLE #25 — Continued

13. The following information must be supplied for each place of business affected by this report.

Name of each establishment and county in which it is located	Type of business, e.g. Manufacturing, Construction, Retail, Wholesale, etc.	Principal Product or Service, e.g. Lumber, Plywood, Plumbing Contractor, Grocery Store, Hotel, Laundry, etc.	Number of Workers 12th of last month
P & P Printing Inc.	retail	printing	none

14. If this report is for an employer of agricultural labor or a private household employing domestic service, indicate the largest amount of payroll in a calendar quarter you have had in either last year or this year.

	Quarter	Year	Payroll Amount
Agricultural Labor			
Domestic Service			

I hereby certify the foregoing statements to be true and correct. To eliminate the need to file duplicate documents, I hereby request the Oregon Department of Revenue to furnish a copy of this report to the Employment Division for registration purposes and a copy to the Workers' Compensation Department for information only.

Date March 16, 19 9- Signed at Portland, Oregon

Signature Jack Printer Signature ______

Signature Jane Printer Signature ______

NOTE: Receipt of this report by the **EMPLOYMENT DIVISION** does not automatically make you liable for taxes under the Employment Division Law. The Division will use the information to determine liability and advise you if liable.

Workers' compensation insurance is mandatory and must be provided by almost every employer. If any doubt exists about your need for this insurance, immediately contact the **WORKERS' COMPENSATION DEPARTMENT** at the number listed below.

NEED MORE INFORMATION?

Oregon Department of Revenue	Employment Division	Workers' Compensation Department
1-800-452-0330	(503) 378-3230	(503) 378-5713

EMPLOYER SHOULD NOT USE SPACE BELOW DOUBLE LINE

A. Codes:
County ______ Industry ______ Audit District ______ By ______

B. Consolidation:
Name of predecessor ______ Reg. No. ______

Successor-in-interest: Yes ______ No ______ By ______ Date ______

History ______

Eligible ______ Tax Rate ______

Ineligible ______ Tax Rate ______ By ______ Date ______

Succeeded by ______ Effective date ______

C. Determination:
(a) Subject ______ Reopened ______ Closed ______ No. of employes ______

(b) Letter to employer: Liab. ______ Ex. ______ By ______ Date ______

Report forms ______ By ______ Date ______

D. Registration completed:
Firm status clearance completed: Date ______ Clearance No. ______ By ______

j. ARRANGE FOR WORKERS' COMPENSATION

Workers' compensation insurance must be carried by every corporation. This applies even though you may have incorporated as an individual and you are the only employee. Workers' compensation insurance provides the corporation with protection against liability from injuries incurred by employees. It also provides for payment of medical and hospital services and compensation for the employees during the time they are unable to work. Briefly stated, workers' compensation insurance covers all employees for injuries received in the course and scope of their employment, regardless of fault.

In the event the corporation does not carry workers' compensation insurance and has made no other provisions for self-insurance, the corporation may become liable for penalties.

Workers' compensation insurance can be purchased from a qualified commercial insurance company or the State Accident Insurance Fund. Employers have the option of providing their own coverage as a self-insured employer, but this is not a practical consideration for small corporations.

Even if you arrange your own private insurance, as an employer you are required to register with the Workers' Compensation Department. This will be done by your insurance company. Be sure you ask them to do this. If you are insuring with the State Accident Insurance Fund in Salem, phone 373-8000 for registration information.

When the employer is registered properly, a Notice of Compliance certificate is issued to the employer. It must be displayed conspicuously in the place of business.

Detailed information about workers' compensation, and the booklet *Oregon Benefits for Injured Workers,* may be obtained by writing to —

Workers' Compensation Department
Labor and Industries Building
Salem, Oregon 97310

k. EMPLOYMENT SECURITY

The Employment Division of the state collects unemployment insurance funds from Oregon employers for the benefit of unemployed workers. The rate varies between 2.2% and 4.0% depending on the claim record of your business. For a new business you are assessed 3.5% on the first $12,000 of wages. The entire cost of unemployment insurance is borne by employers. Even if you are the sole shareholder and employee of your corporation, you will be covered by unemployment insurance. If you are a sole proprietor, however, you are ineligible for coverage.

Warning: Because you wear two hats in this situation (employer and employee), the Employment Division is on the lookout for abuses such as laying yourself off and applying for benefits. So don't do it unless you have a legitimate reason.

Quarterly reports must be filed by the employer. For additional information, contact your local Employment Division office.

l. DO YOU NEED A BUY-SELL AGREEMENT?

A buy-sell agreement is simply an agreement among the shareholders of a corporation that one or more of the shareholders agrees to purchase the shares of the remaining shareholders in the event of a death, resignation, or some other occurrence.

The purpose is to enable the existing shareholders to retain control of the corporation. For example, the death of a shareholder in a "close corporation" or "incorporated partnership" creates a serious situation for both the estate of the deceased shareholder and the surviving shareholders of the corporation.

From the point of view of the estate of the deceased shareholder, the shares of the corporation held by the deceased shareholder may have no market as outsiders will seldom buy such shares unless the business is an established one and they are able to purchase the majority interest in the corporation. The only persons who may be interested in buying the shares may be the surviving shareholders. But if the deceased had a minority interest in the corporation, the surviving shareholders will retain control anyway, so they have no real need to buy the shares. Therefore, they may be able to force the estate to sell the shares at bargain prices.

For a typical close corporation, it may be important to prevent the sale of the shares by the estate to a stranger or to someone with whom the remaining shareholders do not get along, or to prevent the shares being held by the beneficiaries of the deceased shareholder. The death of a shareholder in a close corporation with no prior agreement concerning the disposition of the shares may also adversely affect the credit position of the corporation because of uncertainty as to the future of the business.

The only effective solution to these problems is for all the shareholders of the corporation to enter into a "buy-sell agreement." Under this type of agreement, the estate of a deceased shareholder is obligated to sell and the surviving shareholders are obligated to purchase all of the shares of the deceased at a specified price or at a price to be determined under the agreement. Buy-sell agreements are relatively simple except where there are more than two or three parties. Then this type of agreement can become very complicated.

Buy-sell agreements present two major problems:

(a) The funding of the purchase of the shares

(b) The valuation of the shares of the deceased

Usually, the funds for the purchase of the shares come from business life insurance policies under which each shareholder insures the lives of his or her fellow shareholders, and names himself or herself as the beneficiary of each policy. The idea is that the surviving shareholders will use the insurance proceeds to purchase the shares of the deceased shareholder.

There are, of course, different types of life insurance and the decision as to which type should be obtained by the parties, the amount of insurance, and other related matters should be made only after consultation with an experienced life insurance underwriter. The other problem may be dealt with in a number of ways since no single method of valuation is appropriate to all types of business operations or circumstances.

There are five general methods by which shares can be valued:

(a) By using the valuation imposed by the estate tax authorities

(b) By some form of fixed formula (book value, captalization of earnings, or a combination of two or more of these methods)

(c) By some form of appraisal or arbitration

(d) By a fixed dollar amount by agreement among the parties, with or without a provision for periodic revaluation, or

(e) By a combination of two or more of these methods

The form of buy-sell agreement provided in this book is a very simple one and is provided only as a guide to what might be included (see Sample #26). You should obtain competent legal advice if you wish to enter into a buy-sell agreement unless you are certain of what you are doing.

SAMPLE #26
BUY-SELL AGREEMENT

BETWEEN:

JOHN DOE, Contractor, of 111A Street

in the City of Anywhere, in the State of Oregon;

OF THE FIRST PART

AND:

JACK DOE, Accountant, of 222B Street

in the City of Anywhere, the State of Oregon;

OF THE SECOND PART

(hereinafter collectively called the "shareholders")

WHEREAS:

The shareholders own all the issued and outstanding shares of J & J Personnel Inc. a company incorporated under the laws of the State of Oregon, having its head office in the City of Oregon (hereinafter called the "State of Oregon") and consider it to be advantageous to themselves and to their respective estates to enter into an agreement whereby upon the death of one of them and the survival of the other, the estate of the deceased will be obligated to sell and the survivor will be obligated to purchase the shares owned by the deceased in the corporation; and

The parties wish to assure themselves that when the need arises the survivor will have sufficient monies available to pay, in cash, 1/2 the purchase price for the shares of the deceased;

NOW THEREFORE in consideration of the mutual undertakings of the parties, the parties agree each with the other as follows:

1. On the death of either of the shareholders the survivor will purchase all of the shares owned by the deceased in the corporation and the heirs, executors, administrators, or other legal representatives of the deceased, as the case may be, will sell, convey, and transfer all of the said shares to the survivor on the terms and conditions herein.

2. The purchase price to be paid for the shares as set out in paragraph 1 will be the amount calculated as set out in paragraph 5 (herein called the "calculated value").

3. The survivor will pay the heirs, executors, administrators, or other legal representatives the purchase price as follows:

(a) One-half in cash not later than 60 days after the date appropriate releases are secured to enable the shares to be transferred free and clear of any charge, lien or encumbrance and the proceeds of insurance set out below are received;

(b) the balance thereof in 12 equal installments, the first of which will be paid on the same day of the third month following the date of the first payment and the second and succeeding installments will be paid on the same day of every third month thereafter until such time as the purchase price has been fully paid.

4. The balance of the purchase price outstanding from time to time will bear interest at the rate per annum which is equivalent to 1% per annum in excess of the prime commercial lending rate for the time being charged by Super Savings Bank of Oregon, on loans made by it to prime commercial borrowing customers, such interest to be calculated and be paid at the time of payment of each installment as aforesaid.

SAMPLE #26 — Continued

5. For the purpose of paragraph 2 hereof, the shareholders will cause the duly appointed auditors of the corporation Larry Ledger & Co. , or such other person or persons as the shareholders may in writing agree upon from time to time, to provide the shareholders with a calculated value each year immediately after the completion of the audited financial statements of the corporation. The calculated value will be:

(Here set out the basis for the valuation of the shares. See comments in text on the valuation of shares. Keep in mind that the value may depend on which shareholder has died — particularly in a two- or three-person corporation.)

6. Only annual financial statements which have been approved by each of the shareholders may be used for computing the calculated value.

*7. Each of the shareholders will immediately purchase, and thereafter maintain in good standing, effective life insurance on the life of the other in the amount of $ (insert amount) .

**8. If at any time the calculated value is greater than $100,000 ,each of the shareholders will immediately purchase and maintain such additional life insurance upon the life of the other as is necessary to provide net insurance proceeds equal to the amount that would be payable by the survivor as set out in paragraph 3(a).

9. If either shareholder fails to make any payment required to maintain the life insurance on the other as provided for in the agreement, the other shareholder may make such payment on his or her behalf, and this amount will be payable by the insured immediately to the shareholder making such payment.

10. The parties will cause all policies of insurance on the life of each of the shareholders as provided in paragraphs 7 or 8 to provide that all proceeds will be payable to the other, his or her heirs, executors, and administrators. If any of such life insurance is used, with the written consent of all of the shareholders, as security for any loans or other financial obligations, such policies will be appropriately endorsed as to priority with the proviso that, upon discharge of any such loans or other financial obligation, the whole of the proceeds of the insurance policies will be payable as aforesaid.

11. If, at the time of the death of one of the shareholders, the net proceeds of the insurance payable to the survivor on the death of the deceased are, for any reason, less than the amount required to be paid under paragraph 3(a), the payment required to be made under this paragraph 3(a) will be the amount of the insurance proceeds actually received by the survivor, and the difference between 1/2 the purchase price and the insurance proceeds actually received will be added to the amount to be paid in installments under paragraph 3(b) and the amount of each installment will be increased proportionately.

12. If both of the shareholders should die within 60 days of each other, this agreement will not be operative and the proceeds of all insurance provided for here will be paid to the respective estates of the shareholders.

13. This agreement will terminate automatically if the company is dissolved, wound up, or makes an assignment in bankruptcy, or if a receiving order is made against it under the Bankruptcy Act, or if the company otherwise acknowledges its insolvency. If this agreement is so terminated, each shareholder may, so long as he or she gives notice in writing to the other exercising the rights of assignment within 90 days after the termination of this agreement, receive from the other a full assignment of all the other's rights upon payment to the other of an amount equal to the cash surrender value of the policies of such insurance (if any) and thereafter the insurance will belong solely to the insured.

14. Except by mutual consent of the shareholders, neither of the shareholders may mortgage, charge, hypothecate or otherwise deal with any shares in the company owned by him or her now or hereafter during the continuance of this agreement.

*The amount of life insurance needed is calculated by projecting the calculated value of the shares forward to the next review period (say one year) and dividing the total by the proportionate shareholdings of each individual.

**This clause is to allow for an automatic increase should there be no systematic review of insurance coverage.

SAMPLE #26 — Continued

15. If on the death of one of the shareholders his or her shares are subject to any mortgage, hypothec or lien or any other charge, the survivor may pay the amount required to release the shares, and the heirs, executors, administrators, or other legal representatives of the deceased will reimburse the survivor for such amount on demand.

16. The survivor will not be responsible for the payment of any estate taxes, succession duties, inheritance taxes, or other taxes which may be imposed as a result of the death of the deceased upon the interest of the deceased in the company or upon the proceeds of any insurance policies on the life of the deceased which are subject to this agreement.

17. This agreement will become operative and binding on the shareholders upon delivery by each to the other of certified copies of life insurance policies as provided in clause 7.

18. This agreement will be binding upon and enure to the benefit of the parties hereto and their respective heirs, executors, administrators, and successors.

IN WITNESS WHEREOF the parties have hereunto set their hands and seals this 26th day of May, 19 9- .

SIGNED, SEALED AND DELIVERED
by
in the presence of:

I. M. Witness — John Doe

123 Incorporation Road,
Portland, Oregon

SIGNED, SEALED AND DELIVERED
by
in the presence of:

I. M. Witness — Jack Doe

123 Incorporation Road,
Portland, Oregon

8

TAXES

Unfortunately, the difference between success and failure of a small business too often depends on how well its principal operator takes advantage of the tax laws. A little tax planning now can save a lot of expenditures later.

a. OREGON TAX CONSIDERATIONS

1. State corporate income tax (excise tax)

A corporation is required to pay an annual state income tax imposed by ORS chapter 317. The appropriate forms to file the returns can be obtained from —

State Department of Revenue
State Office Building
P.O. Box 14800
Salem, Oregon 97310

2. Multnomah County business income tax

The state of Oregon collects a business income tax for Multnomah County which is used by the county to provide services to county residents.

Every sole proprietor, partnership, and corporation doing business in Multnomah County must file a return for this tax. The tax is based on the net income from the business within Multnomah County.

For information or forms, contact the Department of Revenue in Salem or a local field office (see page 66).

3. Transit district taxes

The Tri-County Transportation District (Tri-Met) and the Lane County Transit District (LTD) were created to provide revenue for mass transit in those areas. Nearly every employer in the districts must pay the tax that is based on employee wages.

The Tri-Met District includes the Portland area and Clackamas, Multnomah and Washington counties. The LTD includes Eugene and Springfield, and school districts 1, 5J, 68, 69, 71, 154J and a portion of 28J.

The Oregon Department of Revenue provides the forms and collects the funds for these taxes. Employers register for it on the combined form shown in Sample #25 in the last chapter.

b. FEDERAL TAX REGISTRATION REQUIREMENTS

1. Employer identification number

Every new corporation must apply for a federal identification number on IRS Form SS-4 (see Sample #27). Forms are available at any Internal Revenue Service or Social Security Administration office. Internal Revenue also puts out a *Mr. Businessman's Kit,* which should be of great assistance to new businesses as it contains forms for and explanations of how federal taxes are to be remitted.

Every corporation with employees must withhold income and social security taxes from the wages paid to employees.

The amount of withholding tax depends on marital status, number of dependants and rate of pay. The amount of income taxes and social security taxes to be withheld from employees' wages can be determined by using the IRS *Employer's Guide.*

2. Register for social security

Every employee must obtain a social security number by appearing personally

SAMPLE #27
APPLICATION FOR EMPLOYER IDENTIFICATION NUMBER

Form SS–4 (Rev. 8–76)
Department of the Treasury
Internal Revenue Service

Application for Employer Identification Number
(For use by employers and others as explained in the Instructions)

1 Name (True name as distinguished from trade name. If partnership, see Instructions on page 4)
J & J Personnel Incorporated

2 Trade name, if any (Enter name under which business is operated, if different from item 1)
J & J Personnel Inc.

3 Social security number, if sole proprietor

4 Address of principal place of business (Number and street)
123 Incorporator Road,

5 Ending month of accounting year
December

6 City and State
Anywhere, Oregon 97000

7 ZIP code
97000

8 County of business location
Multnomah

9 Type of organization ☐ Governmental (See Instr. on page 4) ☐ Individual ☐ Nonprofit organization (See Instr. on page 4) ☐ Partnership ☒ Corporation ☐ Other (specify)

10 Date you acquired or started this business (Mo., day, year)
May 15, 1978

11 Reason for applying ☒ Started new business ☐ Purchased going business ☐ Other (specify)

12 First date you paid or will pay wages for this business (Mo., day, year)
June 1, 1978

13 Nature of business (See Instructions on page 4)
Employment agency

14 Do you operate more than one place of business? ☐ Yes ☒ No

15 Peak number of employees expected in next 12 months (If none, enter "0") ▶	Nonagricultural	Agricultural	Household
	3	0	0

16 If nature of business is manufacturing, state principal product and raw material used

17 To whom do you sell most of your products or services? ☒ Business establishments ☐ General public ☐ Other (specify)

18 Have you ever applied for an identification number for this or any other business? ☐ Yes ☐ No
If "Yes," enter name and trade name (if any). Also enter the approximate date, city, and State where you first applied and previous number if known. ▶

Date: May 10, 199-
Signature and title: John Doe President
Telephone number: 123-4567

Please leave blank ▶ Geo. | Ind. | Class | Size | Reas. for appl. | **Part I**

at a Social Security Administration office and applying for a number. When starting a new job, every employee must complete an IRS Form W-4 commonly known as the Employee's Withholding Allowance Certificate (see Sample #28). This certificate indicates the employee's marital status and number of dependants. It is used for determining the amount of federal taxes to be withheld from the employee's wages. If an incorporator, director, officer, or shareholder is employed by a corporation and is paid for services performed, he or she is an employee and must have a social security number. All deductions must be withheld as in the case of any other employee.

Sample #28 illustrates the part that is filled in on Form W-4.

The rate of the social security tax to be withheld from each employee's wages is 6.7% of the first $35,700 of wages paid during a calendar year. The employer is required to contribute the same amount of 6.7% of the employee's wages, up to $35,700 of wages paid during the calendar year.

At the end of each year the employer must compute the total compensation paid during the year to each employee, showing the total income tax withheld and the total social security deductions. These figures must be reported on IRS Form W-2 (see Sample #29). The employer must deliver the original and a copy of Form W-2 to each employee. Keep in mind that all federal employee taxes are computed on a calendar year regardless of the corporation's fiscal year.

Note: A W-2 form listing earnings and deductions for the year must be sent to each employee and a W-3 Transmittal Form (see Sample #30) must accompany the W-2 forms sent to the Social Security Administration.

SAMPLE #28
EMPLOYEE'S WITHHOLDING ALLOWANCE CERTIFICATE
(Form W-4)

Form **W-4** (Rev.)
Department of the Treasury
Internal Revenue Service

Employee's Withholding Allowance Certificate

This certificate is for income tax withholding purposes only. It will remain in effect until you change it. If you claim exemption from withholding, you will have to file a new certificate on or before April 30 of next year.

Type or print your full name: Ella Employee

Your social security number: 222-22-2222

Home address (number and street or rural route): 910 Work Street

City or town, State, and ZIP code: Anywhere, Oregon 97123

Marital Status: [X] Single [ ] Married [ ] Married, but withhold at higher Single rate

Note: *If married, but legally separated, or spouse is a nonresident alien, check the single block.*

1 Total number of allowances you are claiming 3
2 Additional amount, if any, you want deducted from each pay (if your employer agrees) . . . . . $ 0
3 I claim exemption from withholding (see instructions). Enter "Exempt" . . . . . nil

Under the penalties of perjury, I certify that the number of withholding exemptions and allowances claimed on this certificate does not exceed the number to which I am entitled. If claiming exemption from withholding, I certify that I incurred no liability for Federal income tax for last year and that I anticipate that I will incur no liability for Federal income tax for this year.

Signature ▶ Ella Employee **Date** ▶ June 1, 19 9-

3. Federal unemployment tax

Every corporation is subject to the federal unemployment tax if it has one or more employees during each 20 calendar weeks in a calendar year or during the preceding year or pays $1,500 or more during any calendar quarter in the current or preceding calendar year. The employer-corporation must pay to the Internal Revenue Service 3.4% of wages paid to employees on the first $8,000 of wages paid during the calendar year. The corporation is permitted to take a credit against its federal unemployment tax for contributions paid into the state unemployment fund of 2.7%. The federal unemployment tax is imposed only on employers and must not be deducted from the wages of employees. The employer must use IRS Form 940 in reporting the unemployment taxes. When the taxes are deposited in an authorized commercial bank or federal reserve bank, the employer must use federal tax deposit Form 508. Form 940 is computed only once a year at the end of the calendar year.

The Internal Revenue Service furnishes guide pamphlets, forms and charts of income and social security taxes to be withheld and other deductions that may be withheld from employees' wages and the amount of contributions to be made by the employer.

4. Filing federal returns and deposits

Each quarter the Internal Revenue Service mails to every corporation IRS Form 941. This is the form used for reporting income and social security taxes withheld and the employer's contribution to the social security fund.

Generally, the employer must deposit the income tax withheld plus the employer's and employee's social security taxes in an authorized commercial bank or a federal reserve bank. In addition to filing the IRS Form 941, the federal tax deposit Form 501 must accompany each Form 941. The computation and requirements for deposits that must be made are printed on the reverse side of IRS Form 941. The amount of taxes to be deposited determines the frequency of deposit.

SAMPLE #29
WAGE AND TAX STATEMENT
(Form W-2)

1 Control number	222	2 Employer's State number		For Official Use Only	
3 Employer's name, address, and ZIP code J & J Personnel Inc. 123 Incorporator Road Anywhere, Oregon 97321		4 Sub-total ☐ Cor-rection ☐ Void ☐ 7 Employer's identification number 00000000		5 Yes ☐ Jan–Mar No ☐ 8 Yes ☐ Jul–Sep No ☐	6 Yes ☐ Apr–Jun No ☐ 9 Yes ☐ Oct–Dec No ☐
10 Employee's social security number 000-00-0000	11 Federal income tax withheld $982.50	12 Wages, tips, other compensation $13,000		13 FICA tax withheld $754.65	14 Total FICA wages $13,000
15 Employee's name (first, middle, last) Ella Employee		16 Pension plan coverage? Yes/No No		17*	18 FICA tips
910 Work Street Anywhere, Oregon 97123 19 Employee's address and ZIP code		20 State income tax withheld $531.02 23 Local income tax withheld		21 State wages, tips, etc. $13,000 24 Local wages, tips, etc.	22 Name of State Oregon 25 Name of locality
Wage and Tax Statement				COPY A For Social Security Administration *See Instructions for Forms W-2 and W-2P and back of Copy D	

Form W–2 Department of the Treasury—Internal Revenue Service

SAMPLE #30
TRANSMITTAL OF INCOME AND TAX STATEMENTS
(Form W-3)

1 Control number	333	2 Employer's State number	For Official Use Only			
Kind of Tax Statements Transmitted	3 Official use	4 Military ☐	5 Agriculture ☐	6 W–2 ☒	7 Original ☒	8 With TIN ☒
	9 Railroad ☐	10 Household ☐	11 State or Local Gov. ☐	12 W–2P ☐	13 Corrected ☐	14 Without TIN ☐
15 State SSA number			16 Number of statements attached 1			17 Date of report 01/22/9-
18 Total FICA tax withheld 754.65			19 Total Federal income tax withheld 982.50			20 Total FICA tips
21 Total FICA wages 13,000			22 Total wages, tips, and other compensation			23 Gross annuities, pensions, retired pay, etc.
24 Employer's identification number 00-0000000				25 Establishment number		26 Taxable annuities, pensions, retired pay, etc.
J & J Personnel Inc. 123 Incorporator Road Anywhere, Oregon 97321 27 Employer's name, address and ZIP code (if available, place label over boxes 24 and 27)				Internal Revenue Service—Department of the Treasury Form **W-3** **Transmittal of Income and Tax Statements**		

Under penalties of perjury, I declare that I have examined this return, including accompanying documents, and to the best of my knowledge and belief, it is true, correct, and complete. In the case of documents without recipients' identifying numbers, I have complied with the requirements of the law by requesting such numbers from the recipients, but did not receive them.

Signature John Doe Title President Date 1/22/9-

5. Federal corporation income tax

All corporations except subchapter S corporations and nonprofit corporations are required to pay federal corporation income tax. The corporation tax is 15% of the first $25,000 net profit. The rate then increases. For example, a corporation earning a net profit of $35,000 will pay 15% of the first $25,000 and 18% of the next $10,000.

The Internal Revenue Service has prepared a booklet entitled *Tax Guide for Small Business.* It is published annually, and you can get one from your post office or by writing to —

Superintendent of Documents
U.S. Government Printing Office
Division of Public Documents
Washington, D.C. 20402

9

HOW TO REGISTER AN OUT-OF-STATE CORPORATION

If you are intending (or already have) started business operations in Oregon as a branch office of a corporation incorporated in another state, you will need to obtain a certificate of authority to do business in Oregon. If you do not, your corporation will not be recognized for purposes of initiating legal action or any other operation that requires you to produce official proof of your ability to carry on business within Oregon, such as obtaining business licenses.

By writing to the Corporation Commissioner, you can get all the necessary documents needed to register your corporation. They are simple to fill out as you can see from Samples #31 and #32.

All foreign corporations are required to maintain a registered office in Oregon and a registered agent at the registered office address. This is required for service of legal documents.

If you have no immediate intention of doing business in Oregon, but would like to protect your corporate name, you may register the name in Oregon by completing an Application for Registration of Corporate Name and filing it with the Corporation Commissioner. The form is free from the Commissioner's office, and the filing fee is $100 per year. You will also need a certificate of good standing from the state in which you are incorporated. This is obtained at the same office where you incorporated (see Sample #33). The registered name is effective for one year.

A foreign corporation intending to apply for a certificate of authority in Oregon may reserve a name by writing to the Corporation Commissioner to request that the name be reserved for 120 days. The fee is $10.

SAMPLE #31
APPLICATION FOR AUTHORITY TO TRANSACT BUSINESS
(Foreign corporation)

Submit the Original and One True Copy with an Original Certificate of Existence (831.115) $440.00

STATE OF OREGON
CORPORATION DIVISION
158 12th Street NE
Salem, OR 97310

Oregon Registry Number:

FOREIGN BUSINESS CORPORATION
APPLICATION FOR AUTHORITY TO TRANSACT BUSINESS

____
(Office Use Only)

PLEASE TYPE OR PRINT LEGIBLY IN BLACK INK

1. Name of the corporation: Western Greenhouses, Inc.

   Note: The name must contain the word "Corporation," "Company," "Incorporated," or "Limited" or an abbreviation of one of such words.

2. State or country of incorporation: Washington

3. Date of incorporation: January 31, 199- Duration, if not perpetual: ______

4. Name of Oregon registered agent: Harvey Gardner

   Address of Oregon registered office (This must be a street address in Oregon which is identical to the registered agent's business office):

567 Dirty Drive	Salem	OREGON	00000
Street and Number	City		Zip Code

5. Address of the principal office of the business: (C/O:) (Attn:) Harvey Gardner

567 Dirty Drive	Salem	Oregon	00000
Street and Number	City	State	Zip Code

6. Mailing address Corporation Division may use for notices (If different from the principal office address):

Street and Number or PO Box	City	State	Zip Code

7. Name and address of president and secretary:

Greta Green	301 Palm Avenue, Olympia, WA
President	Address
Frank Flower	103 Oak Street, Olympia, WA
Secretary	Address

Execution:

	Greta Green	President
Signature	Printed Name	Title

Person to contact about this filing:

Harvey Gardner	000-0000
Name	Daytime Phone Number

Submit the original and a true copy to the Corporation Division, 158 12th Street NE, Salem, OR 97310, with the fee of $400.00 and the surcharge of $40.00 — Total $440.00. Include an ORIGINAL CERTIFICATE OF EXISTENCE, current within 60 days of delivery to this division, uthenticated by the official having custody of the corporate records in the jurisdiction of incorporation. PLEASE DO NOT SEND CASH. If you have questions, call (503) 378-4166.

FBC-1 (6/87) 831.115 ($440.00)

SAMPLE #32
AMENDMENT TO APPLICATION FOR AUTHORITY TO DO BUSINESS
(Foreign corporation)

Submit the Original
And One True Copy
No Fee Required

STATE OF OREGON
CORPORATION DIVISION
158 12th Street NE
Salem, OR 97310

Oregon Registry Number: ____________________
(If known)

FOREIGN CORPORATION
AMENDMENT TO APPLICATION FOR
AUTHORITY TO TRANSACT BUSINESS

PLEASE TYPE OR PRINT LEGIBLY IN BLACK INK

1. The name of the corporation prior to the amendment:

   Western Greenhouses, Inc.

2. The corporate name has been changed to:

   Green Greenhouses of Oregon, Ltd.

3. The duration of the corporation has been changed to:

   [XX] Perpetual

   OR

   [ ] ____________________, ________

   (Please give a specific date.)

Execution: ____________________ Greta Green President
Signature — Printed Name — Title

Person to contact about this filing: Harvey Gardner 000-0000
Name — Daytime Phone Number

Submit the original and a true copy to the Corporation Division, 158 12th Street NE, Salem, Oregon 97310. There is no fee required. If you have questions, please call (503) 378-4166.

FBC-2 (6/87)

SAMPLE #33
CERTIFICATE OF GOOD STANDING

12345

FILE NUMBER

DOMESTIC

THE SEAL OF THE STATE OF WASHINGTON 1889

STATE OF WASHINGTON | DEPARTMENT OF STATE

STATE OF Washington

COUNTY OF Thurston

I HEREBY CERTIFY that according to the records of this office Western Greenhouses Inc. a Corporation duly incorporated under the laws of the State of Washington is an existing Corporation and is with respect to filing of returns, in good standing.

THE SEAL OF THE STATE OF WASHINGTON 1889

In witness whereof I have signed and have affixed the seal of the State of Washington to this certificate at Olympia, the State Capitol,

April 15, 199-

Bruce K. Chapman

BRUCE K. CHAPMAN
SECRETARY OF STATE

10

ANNUAL GENERAL MEETING AND ANNUAL REPORT

a. ANNUAL GENERAL MEETING

Large public corporations have a general meeting of shareholders at least once a year and meetings of directors at regular intervals throughout the year.

Ordinarily, your bylaws will state where the annual meeting of the shareholders and directors will take place (see article 2.3 of Sample #16). If they do not, then the meeting is presumed to be held at the registered office of the corporation.

The time the meeting shall be held should also be stated in the bylaws (see article 2.1 in Sample #16). If the meeting is not held, there is no penalty.

Quite often the minutes of the annual general meeting are simply drawn up by the corporation's attorney to reflect the standard procedures that are usually followed, and are sent to the shareholder/directors of the corporation for their signatures.

The practice of holding imaginary meetings can cause problems if dissension arises later among the shareholders. Then the whole procedure can be attacked. Also, if you are faced with an IRS audit, the IRS agent will usually ask to review your corporate minute book to check the following:

(a) If you are acting like a corporation

(b) If you recorded important events

Without a doubt it is good practice to have an actual meeting at least once a year to review the overall situation. Regardless of whether the business is a corporation or not, a meeting of the owners should be held. Even a sole proprietor can sit down with his or her accountant or lawyer to examine the results of the previous year and make policy decisions for the ensuing year.

Too often a business stagnates and withers away because it lacks direction and purpose. For instance, a retail store goes on selling the same merchandise year after year, ignoring the fact that the competitors are aggressively selling new products. Owners can get so busy running in their well-worn rut that they have no time to look around and examine where they have been or where they are going.

In the other extreme, it is not enough for a businessperson to feel assured that because he or she is constantly alert to all the changes it is unnecessary to stop and consider progress. A change-conscious person who really takes the time to hold a meeting might find that his or her course has been erratic because of a preoccupation with change that has caused a loss of forward direction.

There are also situations where silent partners or minority shareholders never say anything because they are never invited to do so, but they might have some fresh ideas to contribute if given the opportunity.

In contrast, there are minority shareholders who are always complaining about the profit or the general running of the business because they are never informed of the facts. An annual meeting would at least present the time and place to air all of their complaints, and if it is conducted effectively, some positive results might develop to improve the business and so reduce the complaints.

While it is not necessary to run a meeting with full dress formality at a board room table, it does help if there is reasonable order and at least a list of subjects set up as an agenda with one of the persons present appointed as the chairperson to keep the discussion to the point.

Anyone can run a meeting; it does not require an expert. A little practice from attending other meetings which are run in formal order can improve the process immensely.

Be sure that the shareholders elect members of the board of directors. The directors need not be Oregon residents. The board of directors' meeting should follow the shareholders' meeting and elect officers. (The offices such as president and secretary are usually set out in the bylaws — see article 4 of Sample #16).

At the board meeting, the directors should review important events of the past and immediate future. Other items to review in addition to the election of officers include the following:

(a) Salary
(b) Bonuses
(c) Accumulation of surplus
(d) Dividends
(e) Bank resolutions
(f) Medical and dental insurance plans and reimbursement plans
(g) Group life insurance
(h) Fiscal year
(i) Deferred compensation
(j) Major purchases, sales and leases
(k) 1244 corporate resolutions

If the shareholders or the board of directors are in dispute, then the secretary of the corporation should send written notices to all shareholders and directors of the coming meeting more than 10 days before the meeting is scheduled to take place.

The records, minutes, and resolutions of the meeting should be placed in the minute book and kept as a permanent record. Keep them at the principal place of the corporate business.

In order for a meeting of the shareholders of the board of directors to be legal, a quorum must be present. A quorum is usually the majority of shareholders for the shareholder meeting and the majority of the directors for the directors' meeting. This can be changed by the bylaws or in the Articles of Incorporation.

Samples #34 and #35 are the suggested forms for the minutes of the annual meeting of the stockholders and the board of directors.

If you choose not to have a formal meeting, the form shown in Sample #36 illustrates how the shareholders and directors of a company can conduct the usual business by consent of resolution. The resolution, once signed by all directors and shareholders, would then be filed in the minute book.

b. ANNUAL REPORT

Every corporation is required to file an Annual Report and license fee with the Corporation Commissioner. The report and fee are due on the anniversary date (the day each year exactly one or more years after the date on the Certificate of Incorporation). If there is a change of registered agent or office, Form GC-1 (see Sample #37) must also be filed. The annual license fee is $10 (see Table #1).

SAMPLE #34
MINUTES OF SHAREHOLDERS' ANNUAL MEETING

MINUTES OF ANNUAL MEETING OF SHAREHOLDERS

OF

J & J PERSONNEL INC.

The annual meeting of the shareholders was held at the registered office of the Corporation on February 4, 199-

All shareholders were present.

The President gave a report on the business of the Corporation for the preceding year, and after discussion, upon motion duly made, seconded and carried, all actions of the directors were approved, ratified, and confirmed.

The President then called for nominations for directors, and upon motion duly made, seconded and carried, the following were elected directors for the ensuing year:

Jack Doe

John Doe

There being no further business, the meeting was adjourned.

Jack Doe
Secretary-Treasurer

ATTEST:

John Doe
President

SAMPLE #35
MINUTES OF BOARD OF DIRECTORS MEETING

MINUTES OF MEETING OF THE BOARD OF DIRECTORS

OF

J & J PERSONNEL INC.

A meeting of the Board of Directors was held immediately following the annual meeting of shareholders at the registered office of the Corporation on February 4, 199- .

All directors were present.

The President then called for nominations for officers, and upon motion duly made, seconded and carried, the following were elected officers for the ensuing year:

President:	John Doe
Secretary-Treasurer	Jack Doe

There being no further business, the meeting adjourned.

Jack Doe
Secretary-Treasurer

ATTEST:

John Doe
President

SAMPLE #36
WAIVER OF ANNUAL MEETING BY CONSENT RESOLUTION

WAIVER OF ANNUAL MEETING BY CONSENT RESOLUTION

J & J Personnel Inc.

The undersigned, being all shareholders and directors of J & J Personnel Inc., waive the annual general meeting required by Article 2.1 of the Bylaws and consent to the following items of business:

1. That the financial statements prepared and approved by the Corporation's accountant have been presented to each member

2. That the directors of the corporation for the ensuing year be:

   John Doe

   Joe Doe

3. That the officers for the ensuing year be:

   John Doe

   Joe Doe

(OR, in the event of a resignation)

2. That John Doe has tendered his resignation as director effective this date and that Jane Doe was elected as President and director effective this date

3. That the directors of the Corporation for the ensuing year be:

   Jack Doe

   Jane Doe

4. That the officers for the ensuing year be:

   Jack Doe

   Jane Doe

5. That all acts, contracts, proceedings, appointments, and payments of money by the directors and officers of the Corporation since the last annual meeting as appear in proceedings and records of the company be, and the same are, hereby approved, ratified, and confirmed

6. That the directors and officers of the Corporation are instructed to file all necessary reports and documents (This refers to the annual report.)

WE, the shareholders and directors of J & J Personnel Inc. hereby consent to the waiver of this meeting and we consent to the transaction of such business as would have come before it as testified by our signatures hereto this 4th day of February, 199-.

Jack Doe

Jack Doe

John Doe

John Doe

SAMPLE #37
CHANGE OF REGISTERED AGENT AND OFFICE

Submit the Original
No Fee Required

STATE OF OREGON
CORPORATION DIVISION
158 12th Street NE
Salem, OR 97310

Registry Number:

____
(If known)

CHANGE OF REGISTERED AGENT AND OFFICE
Corporations and Business Trusts

PLEASE TYPE OR PRINT LEGIBLY IN BLACK INK

1. Name of corporation: J and J Personnel, Inc.

2. COMPLETE **EITHER** SECTION A, (1)-(6) **OR** SECTION B, (1)-(5) BELOW.

   A. Change of Registered Agent AND Office.

   (1) The registered agent has been changed to: Richard Register

   (2) The new registered agent has consented to this appointment.

   (3) The address of the new registered office is:

   890 Center Street | Anytown | **OREGON** | 00000
   Must be an **Oregon street** address | City | | Zip Code

   (4) The street address of the new registered office and the business address of the new registered agent are identical.

   (5) Mailing address of the registered agent (if different from registered office):

   ____
   Street and Number or PO Box | City | State | Zip Code

   (6) Execution: ______________ | Jay Pumpkin | President
   Signature | Printed Name | Title

   B. Change of Registered Agent's Business Office ONLY.

   (1) The address of the registered office has been changed to:

   ______________ | ______ | **OREGON** | ______
   Must be an **Oregon street** address | City | | Zip Code

   (2) The street address of the new registered office and the business address of the registered agent are identical.

   (3) The corporation has been notified in writing of this change.

   (4) Mailing address of the registered agent (if different from registered office):

   ____
   Street and Number or PO Box | City | State | Zip Code

   (5) Execution: ______________ | ______________ | **Registered Agent**
   Signature of Agent | Printed Name | Title

3. Indicate the address you want the Division to use as a mailing address:

   ☐ A. Please send annual reports to the registered agent.

   ☒ B. Please send annual reports to the corporation at the following address:

   123 First Street | Anytown | Oregon | 00000
   Street and Number or PO Box | City | State | Zip Code

4. Person to contact about this filing: Jay Pumpkin | 000-0000
   Name | Daytime Phone Number

GC-1 (6/87)

11

CORPORATE RULES AND PROCEDURES

a. SHAREHOLDERS' RIGHTS AND RESPONSIBILITIES

There must be an annual meeting of the shareholders, although failure to meet will not necessarily undermine corporate existence. There can be special meetings at any time if proper notification is given by the president, the board of directors, or 10% of the shareholders. Except as limited in the Articles of Incorporation, each outstanding share of voting stock, regardless of class, is entitled to one vote on each matter submitted to a vote at the meeting and may be voted in person or by proxy.

At each annual meeting, the shareholders elect directors to hold office until the next annual meeting and until their successors are elected and qualified. Unless otherwise provided in the Articles of Incorporation, cumulative voting for directors shall be a right of each voting shareholder. This means shareholders have the right to multiply their number of votes by the number of directors to be elected at that meeting and to distribute the total as each sees fit among the candidates.

Unless the articles give the board of directors the power to adopt, alter, or repeal bylaws for regulation of corporate affairs, this power is vested in the shareholders. Also, the power to amend the Articles of Incorporation is absolutely vested in the shareholders, and changes must be approved by holders of two-thirds of all voting shares.

Other major corporate actions that may not be taken by the directors without approval by two-thirds of the shareholders include —

(a) loans by the corporation to its officers or directors,

(b) mergers or consolidations,

(c) sales, lease, exchanges or other disposition of all or substantially all corporate assets, other than in the usual course of business,

(d) voluntary dissolution of the corporation.

A reduction of the stated capital of the corporation may be approved by a simple majority.

It is important to note that shareholder approval means approval at a properly called meeting. However, all actions required to be taken by the voting shareholders may be taken without a meeting if all shareholders consent in writing to not hold the meeting and to the action in question. This is particularly useful in the affairs of closely held corporations.

Account books, minute books, and lists of shareholders are required to be kept by the corporation, and any person who has been a shareholder for at least six months or holds 5% of outstanding shares may inspect these records by giving the corporation at least five days' notice.

b. DIRECTORS' RIGHTS AND RESPONSIBILITIES

Under Oregon law, only one director of the corporation is required. However, it is helpful to have at least three in order to help make decisions and generate ideas. These will normally be the same people who are the shareholders. It is useful to have three directors in order to prevent deadlocks in voting. If you have two directors, one should hold the majority of the shares to avoid similar deadlocks.

The business and affairs of a corporation shall be managed by a board of directors. Business can be transacted at any meeting of the board if a majority of the directors is present. Resolutions may be passed by a majority of those present, once the majority of directors is present. Prior unanimous written consent may replace actions that would be taken at a board meeting.

The board has the sole power to declare dividends from the available earned surplus, from recent net earnings or, on specified occasions, from capital surplus.

If the articles or bylaws allow it, the board may have the power to designate by resolution of a majority of the whole board a committee of its members to exercise the authority of the board on all but the most major corporate actions. However, appointing a committee of directors to oversee day-to-day business does not relieve the board of basic responsibility for corporate management.

The board has the power to elect the corporate officers and to remove any of the officers "whenever in its judgment the best interests of the corporation will be served thereby."

c. REMOVAL OF DIRECTORS

Suppose you are the only shareholder and you elect yourself and two friends to the board of directors. How can they be removed?

The shareholders can hold a special shareholders' meeting at any time, giving proper notice to all shareholders, and at that time, vote to remove any or all of the directors. No reason need be given. Samples #38 and #39 illustrate what you should use to remove directors.

d. OFFICERS

The officers shall consist of a president, one or more vice-presidents, a secretary, and a treasurer. Any two or more offices can be held by the same person unless there is a single shareholder in which case she or he may hold all offices. No officer is required to be a director. However, in most small corporations the directors, officers, and shareholders are all the same people.

Generally the officers' responsibilities are to perform such management duties as provided in the bylaws or as determined by resolution of the board of directors. The officers are subject to removal by the board of directors.

e. TECHNIQUES FOR DIVIDING CORPORATE CONTROL

The division of powers outlined in the corporation statutes seldom coincides precisely with the desires of the organizers of a closely held corporation. Various techniques may be used to more closely reflect the desires of the organizers and major shareholders.

1. Share structure and voting rights

(a) Common and preferred stock

One method of varying the statutory pattern of corporate control is through the use of different classes of stock and by varying the rights within the class. An example is to divide the stock into preferred and common stock. When using preferred stock, the rights, preferences and privileges must be set forth in the Articles of Incorporation. Normally the holder of preferred stock would have specified rights over the holder of common stock. This is usually indicated on the stock certificate itself. For example, a holder of preferred stock may have preferential voting or dividend rights.

(b) Pre-emptive rights

The phrase "pre-emptive rights" refers to the right to retain proportionate ownership in the corporation. This right enables a shareholder to purchase a pro rata portion of most newly authorized stock issued by the corporation, prevent dilution of his or her percentage of ownership and insure a continued ability to elect a portion of the board of directors. Shareholders do not have such pre-emptive rights unless they are granted by the Articles of Incorporation. The desirability of preserving the pro rata ownership of the original investors must be balanced against problems arising when additional capital is sought through the sale of stock.

2. Contracts affecting control

(a) Voting trusts

Any number of shareholders of a corporation may create a voting trust, conferring on a trustee or trustees the right to vote their shares for a period not exceeding 10 years. A copy of the agreement must be filed with the corporation at its registered office. Those signing the voting trust agreement are required to transfer their shares to the named trustee. The transferred certificates are canceled and new certificates are issued to the trustee. It is indicated on the certificates that they are being issued pursuant to the voting trust agreement.

The voting trust agreement may be extended for an additional 10-year period. This device is very powerful and has been upheld even, for example, where the practical effect was to deprive a surviving wife of voting control of community property stock for a period after death.

(b) Shareholder agreements

A shareholder agreement is the ususal method for rearranging the statutory scheme for the management of corporate affairs to meet the desires of the participants. Drafting this agreement may be as important as drafting the Articles of Incorporation and bylaws in forming a closely held corporation. Matters often covered by a shareholder agreement include —

(i) corporate management and variations in voting rights,

(ii) persons to serve as officers and directors,

(iii) employment arrangements and salaries,

(iv) distribution of earnings and timing of possible dividends,

(v) restriction on stock transfers,

(vi) disposition of stock of deceased or disabled stockholders including valuation technique,

(vii) commitments for future financing,

(viii) commitment of certain participants not to acquire, or to have a right to acquire, an interest in certain competing enterprises,

(ix) arrangements concerning purchase of business insurance by the corporation or the participants or combinations thereof,

(x) provisions for arbitration or another method of settling potential deadlocks or disputes.

Generally speaking, an Oregon business corporation may not prevent shareholders from transferring the corporate stock to whomever they wish. However, the modern tendency is to place restrictions on a free transfer if reasonable and if the shareholder acquired the stock with notice of the restriction. Thus, while an outright restriction against transfer may still cause problems of enforceability, restrictions in small corporations may be upheld if a reasonable transfer procedure is provided. A typical device is to provide for first refusal by the corporation, other shareholders or both. Adequate notice of the restrictions must be given. Any limitations on the transferability of the stock to be effective against anyone except persons with actual knowledge of the restriction must be "conspicuously noted" on each certificate.

The shareholder agreement also generally provides for resolution of a "deadlock," and this situation should be defined in the agreement. It may be limited to inability to agree upon matters by a majority of the board of directors or inability to make certain defined significant corporate decisions for a specified period of time. Normally the participants will wish to avoid the provisions of ORS

SAMPLE #38
NOTICE OF SPECIAL MEETING

NOTICE TO SHAREHOLDERS FOR SPECIAL MEETING

TO CONSIDER REMOVAL OF DIRECTORS

To the shareholders of J & J Personnel Inc.

The undersigned shareholders of J & J Personnel Inc. holding 90% of all shares entitled to vote, do hereby call a special meeting of shareholders of J & J Personnel Inc. to be held at 123 Incorporator Road, Anywhere, Oregon, on the 10th day of September, 199-, at 10 o'clock, a.m., for the purposes of considering the removal from office of Dan Director, a member of the Board of Directors.

This notice has been mailed by U.S. Post to the last known address of each shareholder of record.

Date: August 15, 199-

By John Doe

100 shares

57.595 and 57.600, which gives the circuit court power to liquidate the corporation in the event of a deadlock threatening irreparable injury to the corporation. The typical procedure is to agree upon a third party, or a technique for appointing a third party, to serve as an outside director or arbitrator in such a situation.

SAMPLE #39
RESOLUTION REMOVING DIRECTORS

CORPORATE RESOLUTION TO REMOVE DIRECTORS

Meeting of the shareholders was held at 123 Incorporator Rd. Anywhere, Oregon, on the 10th day of September, 199-, at 10 o'clock a.m. for the purposes of considering the removal from office of Dan Director, a member of the Board of Directors.

Upon motion duly made, seconded, and unanimously carried, the following resolution was approved.

RESOLVED: Dan Director, is hereby removed from the Board of Directors of said corporation by the affirmative vote of 600 shares.

Jack Doe
Secretary

Approved by: John Doe

John Doe
President

12

CHANGING YOUR ARTICLES

After your corporation is off and running, the need may arise to amend your articles. In most cases this would be a result of changing the share structure to accommodate additional investors. (See chapter 11 for a discussion of techniques for dividing corporate control.)

To make the change, the board of directors adopts a resolution setting forth the proposed amendment. The amendment is submitted to a vote of the shareholders, either at an annual or a special meeting, after written notice has been given to each shareholder.

After the amendment has been adopted by an affirmative vote of at least a majority of the shares, the Articles of Amendment (see Samples #40 and #41) must be filed with the Corporation Commissioner. Send duplicate originals of the articles. There is no filing fee. The Corporation Commissioner will issue a Certificate of Amendment and return it to you with one of the duplicate originals of the articles.

SAMPLE #40
ARTICLES OF AMENDMENT
(By directors or shareholders)

Submit the Original
And One True Copy
No Fee Required

STATE OF OREGON
CORPORATION DIVISION
158 12th Street NE
Salem, OR 97310

Registry Number:

____
(If known)

ARTICLES OF AMENDMENT
By Directors or Shareholders

PLEASE TYPE OR PRINT LEGIBLY IN BLACK INK

1. Name of the corporation prior to amendment:

   J & J Personnel, Inc.

2. State the article number(s) and set forth the article(s) as it is amended to read. (Attach additional sheets, if necessary.)

   Article IV

   No director shall be personally liable to the corporation or stockholders, subject to any limitations set forth in the Subsection (2)(c) of the Oregon Business Corporation Act.

3. The amendment was adopted on January 10, 19 9-. (If more than one amendment was adopted, identify the date of adoption of each amendment.)

4. Check the **one** appropriate statement:

   ☐ Shareholder action **was not** required to adopt the amendment(s). The amendment was adopted by the board of directors without shareholder action.

   xxx Shareholder action **was** required to adopt the amendment(s). The shareholder vote was as follows:

Class or Series of Shares	Number of Shares Outstanding	Number of Votes Entitled to be Cast	Number of Votes Cast For	Number of Votes Cast Against
Common	1000	1000	1000	None

5. Other provisions, if applicable (Attach additional sheets, if necessary).

Execution: __________ (Signature) John Doe (Printed Name) President (Title)

Person to contact about this filing: John Doe (Name) 000-000 (Daytime Phone Number)

Submit the original and a true copy to the Corporation Division, 158 12th Street NE, Salem, Oregon 97310. There is no fee required. If you have questions, please call (503) 378-4166.

BC-3 (6/87)

SAMPLE #41
ARTICLES OF AMENDMENT
(By incorporators or directors)

Submit the Original
And One True Copy
No Fee Required

STATE OF OREGON
CORPORATION DIVISION
158 12th Street NE
Salem, OR 97310

Registry Number:

____
(If known)

ARTICLES OF AMENDMENT
By Incorporators or Directors

PLEASE TYPE OR PRINT LEGIBLY IN BLACK INK

1. Name of the corporation prior to amendment:

   J and J Personnel, Inc.

2. The corporation has not issued any shares of stock.

3. Shareholder action was not required to adopt the amendment(s). The amendment(s) was adopted by the incorporators or by the board of directors.

4. State the article number(s) and set forth the article(s) as it is amended to read. (Attach additional sheets, if necessary.)

   Article IV

   No holder of shares of stock of the corporation shall be entitled as such as a matter of right to subscribe for, purchase, or otherwise acquire any share of stock of this corporation of any class whether now or hereafter authorized.

5. The amendment was adopted on August 10, 19 9-. (If more than one amendment was adopted, identify the date of adoption of each amendment.)

Execution:

John Doe	John Doe	President
Signature	Printed Name	Title

Person to contact about this filing:

John Doe	000-0000
Name	Daytime Phone Number

Submit the original and a true copy to the Corporation Division, 158 12th Street NE, Salem, OR 97310. There is no fee required. If you have questions, please call (503) 378-4166.

BC-2 (6/87)

13

HOW TO DISSOLVE YOUR CORPORATION

a. OREGON CORPORATIONS

Under the Oregon Business Corporation Act, a corporation can be dissolved by filing the shareholders' consent (see Sample #42) along with duplicate copies of the Articles of Dissolution (see Samples #43 and 44). There is no fee.

When you dissolve your corporation, you must keep in mind that there are other requirements (those imposed by the tax authorites, for example) that must be met. Once your resolution for dissolution is passed, all assets of the corporation should be transferred by deed or written document to their new owners. A dissolved company should own no assets, or future transfer problems could result.

Your corporation will not be dissolved by the Corporation Commissioner until all taxes have been paid.

As far as federal taxes are concerned, the IRS requires you to file Form 966 on ordinary dissolution or liquidation within 30 days of the date you adopted the resolution to dissolve. A certified copy of the resolution (one marked with the corporate seal or, if there is no corporate seal, then a copy that the president and secretary sign as being a true copy of the resolution) must be filed along with the form.

Furthermore, all your quarterly payments of social security or employment insurance should be brought up to date and your final submissions marked as final. Many of the forms you use will have a box or line on them where you can make this statement. You will make the same notation on workers' compensation forms filed with the Department of Labor, and on your city or municipal license forms.

A resolution to dissolve your company cannot be taken lightly. A considerable amount of paper work is required to declare your company legally "dead."

b. OUT-OF-STATE CORPORATIONS

Many of the federal and state tax filings that are required of a local corporation are also required of a "foreign" corporation that did business within the state. For example, you would have to file final employment insurance and workers' compensation payments with the appropriate Oregon agencies.

An Application for Certification of Withdrawal (see Sample #45) would be filed with the Corporation Commissioner, instead of the Articles of Dissolution. As with local corporations, you would make your filing in duplicate. There is no fee.

SAMPLE #42
SHAREHOLDERS' CONSENT

CONSENT

Notice is hereby given that the below noted shareholders of *J & J Personnel Inc.* hereby consent to the voluntary dissolution of the Corporation pursuant to the provisions of ORS 57.536.

Dated this *20th* day of *December*, 199- .

John Doe

John Doe

Jack Doe

Jack Doe

SAMPLE #43
ARTICLES OF DISSOLUTION
(By shareholders)

Submit the Original
And One True Copy
No Fee Required

STATE OF OREGON
CORPORATION DIVISION
158 12th Street NE
Salem, OR 97310

Registry Number:

____
(If known)

ARTICLES OF DISSOLUTION
By Shareholders

PLEASE TYPE OR PRINT LEGIBLY IN BLACK INK

1. Name of the corporation: J & J Personnel, Inc.

2. Date dissolution was authorized: January 10, 199-

3. Shareholder vote on the resolution to dissolve was as follows:

Class or Series of Shares	Number of Votes Entitled to be Cast	Number of Votes Cast For	Number of Votes Cast Against
Common	1000	1000	None

4. The number of votes cast in favor of dissolution was sufficient for approval.

Execution: John Doe (Signature) John Doe (Printed Name) President (Title)

Person to contact about this filing: John Doe (Name) 000-0000 (Daytime Phone Number)

Submit the original and a true copy to the Corporation Division, 158 12th Street NE, Salem, OR 97310. There is no fee required. If you have questions, please call (503) 378-4166.

BC-7 (6/87)

SAMPLE #44
ARTICLES OF DISSOLUTION
(By incorporators or initial directors)

Submit the Original
And One True Copy
No Fee Required

STATE OF OREGON
CORPORATION DIVISION
158 12th Street NE
Salem, OR 97310

Registry Number:

____
(If known)

ARTICLES OF DISSOLUTION
By Incorporators or Initial Directors

PLEASE TYPE OR PRINT LEGIBLY IN BLACK INK

1. Name of the corporation: J and J Personnel, Inc.

2. Date of Incorporation: August 15, 199-

3. None of the corporation's shares have been issued and the corporation has not commenced business.

4. No debt of the corporation remains unpaid.

5. A majority of the incorporators or initial directors authorized this dissolution.

Execution:	John Doe	John Doe	President
	Signature	Printed Name	Title

Person to contact about this filing:	John Doe	000-0000
	Name	Daytime Phone Number

Submit the original and a true copy to the Corporation Division, 158 12th Street NE, Salem, OR 97310. There is no fee required. If you have questions, please call (503) 378-4166.

BC-6 (6/87)

SAMPLE #45
FOREIGN CORPORATION WITHDRAWAL OF AUTHORITY TO TRANSACT BUSINESS

Submit the Original
And One True Copy
No Fee Required

STATE OF OREGON
CORPORATION DIVISION
158 12th Street NE
Salem, OR 97310

Oregon Registry Number:

____
(If known)

FOREIGN CORPORATION
WITHDRAWAL OF AUTHORITY
TO TRANSACT BUSINESS

PLEASE TYPE OR PRINT LEGIBLY IN BLACK INK

1. The name of the corporation: Green Greenhouses of Oregon, Ltd.

2. State or country of incorporation: Washington

3. This corporation is not transacting business in Oregon, and surrenders its authority to transact business in Oregon.

4. This corporation revokes the authority of its registered agent to accept service on its behalf and appoints the Corporation Division as its agent for service of process in any proceeding based on a cause of action arising during the time it was authorized to transact business in Oregon.

5. Mailing address to which the person initiating any proceeding may mail to this corporation a copy of any process served on the Corporation Division:

1234 S. Sandy Blvd.	Olympia	Washington	98000
Street and Number or PO Box	City	State	Zip Code

The corporation will notify the Corporation Division of any change in this mailing address for a period of five years from the date of this withdrawal.

Execution:	Frank Flower	Frank Flower	President
	Signature	Printed Name	Title

Person to contact about this filing:	Greta Green	000-0000
	Name	Daytime Phone Number

Submit the original and a true copy to the Corporation Division, 158 12th Street NE, Salem, OR 97310. There is no fee required. If you have questions, please call (503) 378-4166.

FBC-3 (6/87)

APPENDIX

DETAILED CHECKLIST OF STEPS TO BE FOLLOWED IN INCORPORATION

_________ Name decided on

_________ Phoned Corporation Commissioner to clear name

_________ Letter and fee to the Corporation Commissioner to reserve name

_________ Package forms ordered

_________ Articles prepared

_________ Documents forwarded to Corporation Commissioner
(i) Duplicate copies of Articles of Incorporation
(ii) Check (certified) payable to Corporation Commissioner in the amount calculated from Table #1.

_________ Incorporation documents received back from Salem

_________ Minute book purchased

_________ Seal ordered (not mandatory)

_________ Banking resolutions completed and account opened

_________ Minutes of various meetings drawn and signed:
(i) Organizational meeting of directors
(ii) Meeting of shareholders

_________ Share certificates issued

_________ Minute book opened and originals of minutes and copies of all other documents inserted in chronological order

_________ Miscellaneous steps:
(i) Assets transferred to company by drafting minutes, etc.
(ii) Subsection S and plan 1244 steps taken
(iii) If motor vehicle(s) involved, Department of Motor Vehicles contacted for transfer purposes

_________ Annual Report filed

GLOSSARY

CORPORATION TERMS

Before attempting to form your own close corporation, you should become familiar with the following fundamental corporation terms and their meanings.

ARTICLES OF INCORPORATION
The instrument by which a corporation is formed and organized under general corporation laws

BOARD OF DIRECTORS
The governing body of a corporation

BYLAWS
Rules for governing the internal affairs of a corporation

CERTIFICATE STOCK
also called share certificate
A certificate of the corporation in which a person is named as the owner of a designated number of shares of stock

CHARITABLE CORPORATION
A corporation having the character or purpose of providing charity. It is usually a nonprofit corporation also known as an eleemosynary corporation.

CLOSE CORPORATION
An Oregon corporation consisting of a minimum of one incorporator and a maximum of 50 shareholders, and having restrictions on share transfers

CORPORATION
A legal entity and an artificial or fictitious person organized for the purpose of doing business within a state when its Articles of Incorporation are filed

De Facto CORPORATION
A business organization which operates as a corporation but which has failed to comply with one or more of the provisions of state law regarding the organization of a corporation

De Jure CORPORATION
A corporation which complies completely with the corporate laws of the state in which it is formed

DIRECTOR
One who has been elected or appointed to the board of directors

MEETING
Assembling of the board of directors or shareholders for the purpose of transacting business

MINUTES OF MEETING
The record of the business transacted at a meeting

OFFICER
An elected official of the corporation, such as president, vice president, secretary, or treasurer

PRIVATE CORPORATION
A corporation organized for the purpose of engaging in a business, earning a profit, and paying dividends to shareholders

PROXY
An authorization in writing signed by a shareholder designating another person to vote in his or her place

PUBLIC CORPORATION
An entity organized for governmental purposes, such as county or city governments

QUORUM
The number of members of the board of directors, committee or other organized body required to make that body, when duly assembled, legally competent to transact business

SHAREHOLDER
The owner of stock in a corporation

STOCK
The certificate or evidence of ownership of an interest in a corporation

Ultra Vires ACT
An act beyond the powers conferred upon a corporation by its Articles of Incorporation

WAIVER OF NOTICE AND CONSENT
An instrument which waives notice of a special meeting and consents to the holding of the meeting and transaction of business. It is signed by members of the board of directors and may be used by shareholders at a special meeting.

OTHER TITLES IN THE SELF-COUNSEL BUSINESS SERIES

STARTING A SUCCESSFUL BUSINESS ON THE WEST COAST
by Douglas L. Clark

Create your own job in California, Oregon, or Washington!

With a swelling population and increased trade among Pacific Rim countries, future opportunities for the West Coast look even brighter.

Here is a book that gives entrepreneurs what they need the most — practical advice, usable information, and solid tips on the best ways to establish a business. Written specifically for first-time businesspeople in California, Oregon, and Washington, the book offers an abundance of information that will prove of continuing value to the new business operator. $14.95

Packed with practical advice and money-saving tips, this book shows you how to start and operate your own successful business on the West Coast. Here are a few of the topics it covers:

- Deciding how to organize your business
- Coping with federal, state, and local laws
- Finding the best location
- How to save money when setting up your business
- How and where to get financing
- How to get help from the government
- Using tax laws to your advantage
- Buying a business or a franchise
- How to find and keep good employees
- How to set up and maintain proper records

GETTING-INTO-BUSINESS GUIDES
by Dan Kennedy

Ideas, information, and inspiration to help small businesses get a running start at success. These four books, available individually or as a boxed set, cover information every aspiring entrepreneur should know before getting into business. Boxed set, $29.95

GETTING READY
This book helps prospective entrepreneurs determine whether their business plan is workable and if they have the right qualities to see the idea through to fruition. It lists the traits shared by most winning business people and helps people decide what the best type of business is for them, based on their individual strengths. $7.95

GETTING STARTED
This guide details all the practical aspects of starting a business. It examines the pros and cons of incorporation and proprietorship, finding the best location for a business, and choosing and registering a memorable company name. $7.95

GETTING MONEY
This fundamental guide provides readers with an understanding of the traditional and non-traditional funding sources available. It shows where and how a new business can find start-up capital and establish credit. $7.95

GETTING SALES
An invaluable guide that explains the rules of small business sales and marketing in a clear, understandable form. It illustrates key marketing strategies that enable a product or service business to identify, target, and sell to its ideal market. $7.95

START AND RUN SERIES

START AND RUN A PROFITABLE BED AND BREAKFAST

by Monica and Richard Taylor

This book shows you the business side of opening your home to visitors. The clearly written text along with dozens of worksheets and explanatory samples show you how to plan everything from renovations to recordkeeping and how to keep your business running trouble-free through its first few years. $14.95

START AND RUN A PROFITABLE CONSULTING BUSINESS

by Douglas Gray, B.A., LL.B.

This practical step-by-step success guide shows how anyone can turn their knowledge and experience into a profitable consulting business. The comprehensive discussions on all aspects of consulting will get you over the first hurdle of starting your business and direct you toward a successful and profitable marketing plan. $14.95

START AND RUN A PROFITABLE CRAFT BUSINESS

by William G. Hynes, Ph.D.

This book is for anyone who has ever considered taking up crafts or who is already involved in crafts as a hobby or business. Those who want to turn their hobby into a money-making project and those who want to improve their current sales will benefit from the dozens of tips in this book. It gives practical instructions for setting up and operating a successful craft business, whether it is done from the kitchen table or a production workshop. $12.95

START AND RUN A PROFITABLE HOME-BASED BUSINESS

by Edna Sheedy

Do you fantasize about getting up in the morning and stepping into your office without ever stepping outside? $12.95

If this is your favorite daydream, this book will help you turn it into reality. In lively language, the author answers questions such as:

- What are the legal requirements of a home-based business?
- How do I run my business without disrupting my family?
- What professional advice will I need and where will I get it?

START AND RUN A PROFITABLE RESTAURANT

by Michael M. Coltman, M.B.A., C.G.A.

This book provides all the information you need to get started and make a profit in the restaurant business. It takes you step by step through the process and shares tips from the experts so you can avoid the mistakes that so many restaurateurs make. $12.95

START AND RUN A PROFITABLE RETAIL BUSINESS

by Michael M. Coltman, M.B.A., C.G.A.

Opening a retail store or service business is a very different venture than starting other kinds of businesses. This book specifically deals with the unique problems and opportunities of small retailers. $12.95

Some of the questions it answers are:

- How do I find the right location?
- Is franchising a good idea?
- What do I do about record keeping and accounts?

PREPARING A SUCCESSFUL BUSINESS PLAN

A practical guide for small business

by Rodger Touchie

At some time, every business needs a formal business plan. Whether considering a new business venture or rethinking an existing one, an effective plan is essential to success. From start to finish, this working guide outlines how to prepare a plan that will win potential investors and help achieve business goals.

Using worksheets and a sample plan, readers learn how to create an effective plan, establish planning and maintenance methods, and update their strategy in response to actual business conditions. $14.95

Contents include:

- The basic elements of business planning
- The company and its product
- The marketing plan
- The financial plan
- The team
- Concluding remarks and appendixes
- The executive summary
- Presenting an impressive document
- Common misconceptions in business planning
- Your business plan as a tangible asset

KEEPING CUSTOMERS HAPPY

Strategies for success

by Jacqueline Dunckel and Brian Taylor

Customer satisfaction is your company's best asset!

Consumers today demand personal attention from businesses before they spend their money. So, customer service is moving up the priority list in dynamic companies and it is consuming more of their time and budgets; businesses that ignore customer relations do so at their peril.

You need good service to attract customers and keep them coming back, and this book provides plans and programs that have been proven successful by other businesses. No matter what kind of business you are in, this book will help increase profits through improved customer relations. $8.95

Contents include:

- Customer service — what it is and what it is not
- The "why" of customer relations
- The value of service
- Developing a profitable customer relations program
- Setting goals for your business
- Putting your plan together
- Communicating your customer relations program to your employees
- Training employees
- Bringing it all together

STANDARD LEGAL FORMS AND AGREEMENTS
Steve Sanderson, editor

This book provides a wide selection of indispensable legal forms and common business agreements ready to be copied and filled in with the particulars of the arrangement. It features a lay-flat binding and all samples are provided full-size in this large format volume so that no fussing with enlargements is necessary and copying is both easy and perfect quality. $14.95

- New businesses — agreement of purchase — partnership agreement
- Services — engagement of services
- Employment — employment agreement — employee dismissal letter
- Buying — invitation to quote — cancellation of purchase order
- Selling — bill of sale — limited warranty
- Collections — request for payment — bad check letter
- Credit/Debit — personal credit application — guarantee
- Leases — commercial lease — agreement to cancel lease
- Assignments — assignment with warranties

ORDER FORM

All prices are subject to change without notice. Books are available in book, department, and stationery stores. If you cannot buy the book through a store, please use this order form. (Please print)

Name_______________________________

Address_____________________________

____

Charge to:

❑Visa ❑ MasterCard

Account Number____________________

Validation Date ____________________

Expiry Date________________________

Signature__________________________

❑**Check here for a free catalog outlining all of our publications.**

Please send your order to
Self-Counsel Press Inc.
1704 N. State Street
Bellingham, WA 98225

YES, please send me:

_____copies of **Starting a Successful Business on the West Coast**, $14.95

_____copies of **Getting-Into-Business Guides**, Boxed set of 4, $29.95

_____copies of **Getting Ready**, $7.95

_____copies of **Getting Started**, $7.95

_____copies of **Getting Money**, $7.95

_____copies of **Getting Sales**, $7.95

_____copies of **Start and Run a Profitable Bed and Breakfast**, $14.95

_____copies of **Start and Run a Profitable Consulting Business**, $14.95

_____copies of **Start and Run a Profitable Craft Business**, $12.95

_____copies of **Start and Run a Profitable Home-Based Business**, $12.95

_____copies of **Start and Run a Profitable Restaurant**, $12.95

_____copies of **Start and Run a Profitable Retail Business**, $12.95

_____copies of **Preparing a Successful Business Plan**, $14.95

_____copies of **Keeping Customers Happy**, $8.95

_____copies of **Standard Legal Forms and Agreements**, $14.95

Please add $2.50 for postage & handling.